THE STORY OF THE BIBLE

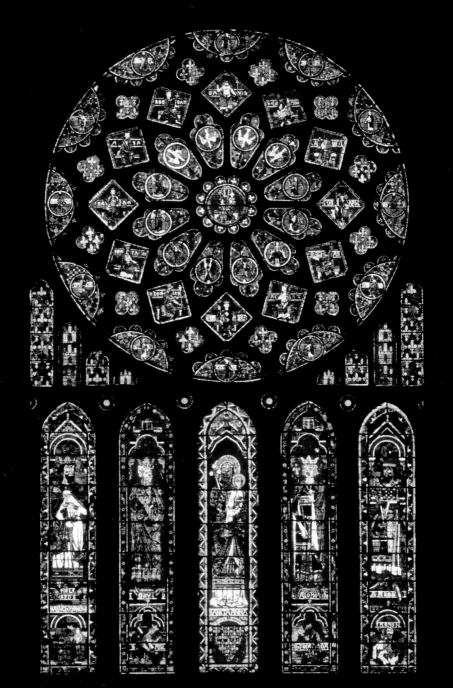

THE STORY
OF THE
BIBLE

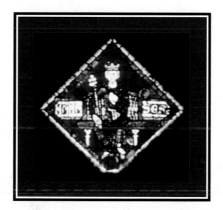

IDEALS PUBLICATIONS
NASHVILLE, TENNESSEE

ISBN 0-8249-5843-8

Library of Congress Cataloging-in-Publication Data
The story of the Bible.
        p.   cm.
    1. Bible—Introductions.   I. Ideals Publications
Incorporated.
BS475.2.S78   1998
220—dc21   948-12265
                                    CIP

Printed and bound in Italy
Color separations by Precision Color Graphics,
Franklin, Wisconsin

10 9 8 7 6 5 4 3 2

Publisher, Patricia A. Pingry
Associate Editors, Michelle Prater Burke,
    Nancy Skarmeas
Designer, Eve DeGrie
Managing Editor, Peggy Schaefer
Production Artist, Patrick McRae
Copy Editor, Amy Johnson
Editorial Consultant, James F. Couch, Jr.

Cover photographs (from left to right): painting of Peter by Peter Paul Reubens, Superstock; *Moses with the Tablets of the Law* by Rembrandt van Rijn, Dahlem Staatliche Gemaldegalerie, Berlin/Bridgeman Art Library, London/Superstock; painting of the apostle Paul by Rembrandt van Rijn, Kunsthistorisches, Vienna/A.K.G., Berlin/Superstock.

Published by Ideals Publications
A division of Guideposts
535 Metroplex Drive, Suite 250
Nashville, Tennessee 37211
www.idealsbooks.com

ACKNOWLEDGMENTS

Barclay, William. Excerpt from *The Master's Men,* copyright © 1959 by William Barclay. Used by permission of SCM Press, Ltd., London.
Josephus, Flavius. Excerpts from *The Life and Words of Flavius Josephus.*
Keller, Werner. Excerpts from *The Bible as History,* copyright 1956 by Werner Keller. Used by permission of William Morrow.
Phillips, J. B. Excerpt from *Ring of Truth,* copyright © 1967 by J. B. Phillips. Used by permission of Hodder and Stoughton Ltd., London.
Potok, Chaim. Excerpts from *Wanderings,* copyright © 1978 by Chaim Potok. Used by permission of Random House, Inc.
Schaeffer, Francis A. Excerpts from *Joshua and the Flow of Biblical History,* copyright © 1975 by L'Abri Fellowship. Used by permission of L'Abri Fellowship.
Wieder, Laurance. Excerpt from the introduction to *The Poets' Book of Psalms,* edited by Laurance Wieder, copyright © 1995 by Laurance Wieder, used by permission of the author.

CONTENTS

THE
EARLIEST
SCRIPTURES

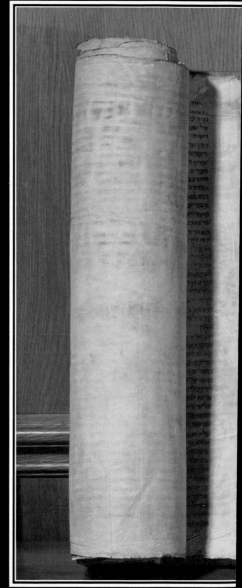

*Pictured at right are manuscripts of the
Hebrew Pentateuch, the first five books of
the Bible, which are also called the Torah.*

THE BEGINNING

The Bible opens with the Book of Genesis, a Greek word that means "origin" or "beginning." The original Hebrew title, Bereshith, literally means "in the beginning," which are the first words of the Bible: "In the beginning, God . . ." Genesis spans more time than any other book of the Bible, covering more than all the remaining sixty-five books combined and ending some three centuries before the birth of Moses. But it is Moses who is credited as the author not only of Genesis but of the first five books of the Bible, called the Pentateuch.

Genesis sets the stage for the rest of the Bible and provides its coherence as a total work. The literary structure of this first book is built around eleven separate units, each of which begins with a phrase containing the word *generation*. We are told about the beginning of man, his lineage, and his fall, but we are also told of the lineage of the Saviour to come. Adam enters the world sinless, like Christ, through a special act of God. Abel's blood sacrifice mirrors Christ's sacrifice. Adam becomes the head of the old creation whereas Christ is the head of the new creation. This theme continues throughout Genesis and throughout the Bible. Christ is the seed of woman (3:15), from the line of Seth (4:25), the son of Shem (9:27), the descendant of Abraham (12:3), of Isaac (21:12), of Jacob (25:23), and of the tribe of Judah (49:10).

Genesis is not just the history of man, it is the history of the redemption of man. God is the sovereign Creator of all things in space and time, and man is His ultimate creation. But through sin, man is separated from God. As man multiplies, sin also multiplies until God is forced to destroy the world through the flood, saving only Noah and his family.

After the nations scatter because of the rebellion at the tower of Babel, God focuses His attention on one man, Abraham, and his descendants, through whom God will bless all mankind. God makes His covenant with Abraham, establishes a spiritual link with Isaac, and transforms Jacob and changes his name to Israel. Jacob becomes the father of twelve sons, one of whom, Joseph, is sold into slavery in Egypt. Joseph becomes ruler in Egypt and delivers his family from famine by bringing them to Egypt. Genesis ends with the death of Joseph and the need for redemption that is to follow.

Pictured at left is the painting The Garden of Eden *by Flemish artist Jan Brueghel the Elder.*

MOSES

oses was born in Egypt in secret, the younger of the two sons of a Levite couple. His mother kept him hidden to protect him until the child grew too old to hide. She then placed the baby in a basket among the bulrushes along the Nile. The basket was discovered by a daughter of the Pharaoh, who took pity on the baby and raised him as her own.

The sister of Moses, Miriam, saw the daughter of the Pharaoh take the child out of his hiding place and rushed up to offer herself and Moses' mother as nurses. Moses was raised as the grandson of the Pharaoh yet overseen by his own mother.

As an adult, Moses killed an Egyptian who was beating a Hebrew slave. When word of the murder became known, Moses fled for his life to Midian, where he married Zipporah, the daughter of a Midianite priest.

While Moses was tending his father-in-law's sheep, God revealed Himself to Moses in the burning bush. God told Moses to return to Egypt and lead the Jews out of slavery. With his brother Aaron's help, he went to Pharaoh who, after nine plagues sent by God, still refused to release the Hebrews. The tenth plague, the slaughter of the first-born, convinced Pharaoh to let them go.

Moses led the people across the Red Sea, which divided to let them pass and closed only after the Egyptian soldiers had entered the waters. Crossing the Sinai Desert, Moses received God's law, written upon the tablets of stone. Moses, however, was not allowed to enter the Promised Land. That privilege of leading the band of Hebrews to Canaan was reserved for his successor, Joshua.

Pictured above is a detail of a wall painting in the tomb of the Pharaohs who ruled during the fifteenth century B.C. In the painting, craftsmen lay bricks and build pylons, much like the work of the Hebrews during their captivity in Egypt.

Pictured at left is a detail of a wall painting in the tomb of Mennah, scribe of the fields and estate inspector under Pharaoh Thutmosis IV. An Egyptian overseer beats a slave, perhaps a Hebrew. Such a sight caused Moses to lose his temper and kill an Egyptian overseer.

THE CALLING OF MOSES

And it came to pass in process of time, that the king of Egypt died: and the children of Israel sighed by reason of the bondage, and they cried, and their cry came up unto God by reason of the bondage. And God heard their groaning, and God remembered his covenant with Abraham, with Isaac, and with Jacob. And God looked upon the children of Israel, and God had respect unto them.

Now Moses kept the flock of Jethro his father-in-law, the priest of Midian: and he led the flock to the backside of the desert, and came to the mountain of God, even to Horeb. And the angel of the LORD appeared unto him in a flame of fire out of the midst of a bush: and he looked, and, behold, the bush burned with fire, and the bush was not consumed.

And Moses said, I will now turn aside, and see this great sight, why the bush is not burnt.

And when the LORD saw that he turned aside to see, God called unto him out of the midst of the bush, and said, Moses, Moses. And he said, Here am I.

And He said, Draw not nigh hither: put off thy shoes from off thy feet, for the place whereon thou standest is holy ground.

Moreover He said, I am the God of thy father, the God of Abraham, the God of Isaac, and the God of Jacob. And Moses hid his face; for he was afraid to look upon God.

And the LORD said, I have surely seen the affliction of my people which are in Egypt, and have heard their cry by reason of their taskmasters; for I know their sorrows;

And I am come down to deliver them out of the hand of the Egyptians, and to bring them up out of that land unto a good land and a large, unto a land flowing with milk and honey; unto the place of the Canaanites, and the Hittites, and the Amorites, and the Perizzites, and the Hivites, and the Jebusites. Now therefore, behold, the cry of the children of Israel is come unto me: and I have also seen the oppression wherewith the Egyptians oppress them. Come now therefore, and I will send thee unto Pharaoh, that thou mayest bring forth my people the children of Israel out of Egypt.

And Moses said unto God, Who am I, that I should go unto Pharaoh, and that I should bring forth the children of Israel out of Egypt?

And He said, Certainly I will be with thee; and this shall be a token unto thee, that I have sent thee: When thou hast brought forth the people out of Egypt, ye shall serve God upon this mountain.

And Moses said unto God, Behold, when I come unto the children of Israel, and shall say unto them, The God of your fathers hath sent me unto you; and they shall say to me, What is His name? what shall I say unto them? And God said unto Moses, I AM THAT I AM: and He said, Thus shalt thou say unto the children of Israel, I AM hath sent me unto you. And God said moreover unto Moses, Thus shalt thou say unto the children of Israel, The LORD God of your fathers, the God of Abraham, the God of Isaac, and the God of Jacob, hath sent me unto you: this is my name for ever, and this is my memorial unto all generations. Go, and gather the elders of Israel together, and say unto them, The LORD God of your fathers, the God of Abraham, of Isaac, and of Jacob, appeared unto me, saying, I have surely visited you, and seen that which is done to you in Egypt:

And I have said, I will bring you up out of the affliction of Egypt unto the land of the Canaanites, and the Hittites, and the Amorites, and the Perizzites, and the Hivites, and the Jebusites, unto a land flowing with milk and honey (Exodus 2:23–3:17).

THE FIRST SCRIPTURES

Moses is credited as the author of the first five books of the Bible: Genesis, Exodus, Leviticus, Numbers, and Deuteronomy. The Bible is replete with testimonies to Moses as author, both in the Old Testament and in the New Testament. The early church held to the Mosaic authorship, as does

In ancient Egypt, scribes copied information from small tablets onto larger clay tablets. After the clay tablets were baked, they were stored on shelves in archives as permanent files. These file tablets measured about twelve by eight inches. Pictured at left is one of fifteen thousand tablets in the Royal Archives (2400 B.C.), which were excavated in 1975 in Ebla, Syria.

the first-century Jewish historian Flavius Josephus. Orthodox Jews believe that the Torah was literally dictated by God to Moses on top of Mt. Sinai.

A few scholars question whether or not Moses had the tools with which to write. Jesus, however, cited Moses as the author of the Pentateuch, as expressed in the Gospel of Matthew: "And Jesus saith unto him, See thou tell no man; but go thy way, show thyself to the priest, and offer the gift that Moses commanded, for a testimony unto them" (Matthew 8:4).

Luke also named Moses as the author of the first five books of the Bible in Luke 24:27: "And beginning at Moses and all the

Pictured at right is the profile of a bust of Queen Nefertiti, the Egyptian Queen during the first half of the fourteenth century B.C.

prophets, he expounded unto them in all the scriptures the things concerning himself."

And Paul recognized Moses as author in Paul's Second Letter to the Corinthians (3:15): "But even unto this day, when Moses is read, the veil is upon their heart."

A discovery was made in 1887 which shows that Moses could very well have written the Scriptures. An Egyptian woman from the fellaheen community of Tell el-Amarna stumbled upon clay tablets buried beneath the ruins of an ancient mudbrick building behind her village. The tablets were from the Egyptian Royal Archives. Archaeologists uncovered more than three hundred and eighty tablets, which are now housed in museums in Berlin, London, and Cairo.

These documents are mostly written in cuneiform, which are wedge-shaped "sign groups." The tablets were letters sent to Egypt from city-state rulers and, incredibly, even included file copies of the replies of Pharaoh. Also found was correspondence from the great kings of the powerful northern kingdoms of Mitanni, Hatti (Turkey), Alashiya (Cyprus), Karduniash (Babylonia), and Assyria. Once the letters arrived in Egypt, they were sent to Amarna to be translated by the scribes and then to Pharaoh and his advisers. The tablets were stored in the House of Correspondence of Pharaoh, where they were found some three thousand years later. Because of this discovery, we now know that Moses, fifteen hundred years before Christ, could very well have actually written the first five books of the Bible.

The Pentateuch contains the laws laid out by God to man, the moral code that became the basis for the law of most of today's civilizations. These first five books of the Bible tell us about God's creation and then destruction of the world by the flood. They describe God's covenant with Abraham and the history of the enslavement of the Jews in Egypt, their subsequent exodus, and their journey to the border of the Promised Land. With God's guidance, Moses not only laid the foundation for an emerging nation but, more importantly, prepared the way for the coming Messiah.

In Genesis, in the account of the forty-year-long wandering through the desert, we at last read of how the first Scriptures were given to man by God on top of Mt. Sinai. After crossing the Red Sea, Moses and his followers could have taken any one of the four established trade routes through the Sinai Desert. The northern route would have taken them straight to a line of Egyptian fortresses and thus into armed conflict. Two of the other routes across Sinai cross right through the center of the peninsula, a hard and difficult road through uninhabitable terrain. The fourth trade route roughly followed the coastline southward, passing the mountain of Santa Katerina. Scholars often identify this mountain as the Mt. Sinai of the Bible although there are other possibilities, one of which is the mountain Jebel Musa, farther to the north. Since the Egyptians never ventured into the southern part of the Sinai Peninsula, most scholars believe that this southern route is the most likely for the escaping Jews.

It seems incredible that, although Mt. Sinai figures so prominently in the Scriptures and remains important to us today, Jewish tradition offers no clues as to its whereabouts. It was not a place of pilgrimage for the early Jews, and Jewish tradition has no memory of the site. The newcomers to the land of Canaan were interested in preserving their existence and carving out a home, and their religious beliefs seemed to have been linked to Jerusalem and the Tabernacle.

Pictured below is a view of the Red Sea as seen from the Sinai Peninsula.

THE TEN COMMANDMENTS

In the third month, when the children of Israel were gone forth out of the land of Egypt, the same day came they into the wilderness of Sinai. . . . And mount Sinai was altogether on a smoke, because the LORD descended upon it in fire: and the smoke thereof ascended as the smoke of a furnace, and the whole mount quaked greatly. And the LORD called Moses up to the top of the mount; and Moses went up.

And God spake all these words, saying, I am the LORD thy God, which have brought thee out of the land of Egypt, out of the house of bondage.

Thou shalt have no other gods before me.

Thou shalt not make unto thee any graven image, or any likeness of any thing that is in heaven above, or that is in the earth beneath, or that is in the water under the earth:

Thou shalt not bow down thyself to them, nor serve them: for I the LORD thy God am a jealous God, visiting the iniquity of the fathers upon the children unto the third and fourth generation of them that hate me; And shewing mercy unto thousands of them that love me, and keep my commandments.

Thou shalt not take the name of the LORD thy God in vain; for the LORD will not hold him guiltless that taketh his name in vain.

Remember the sabbath day, to keep it holy. Six days shalt thou labour, and do all thy work: But the seventh day is the sabbath of the LORD thy God: in it thou shalt not do any work, thou, nor thy son, nor thy daughter, thy manservant, nor thy maidservant, nor thy cattle, nor thy stranger that is within thy gates: For in six days the LORD made heaven and earth, the sea, and all that in them is, and rested the seventh day: wherefore the LORD blessed the sabbath day, and hallowed it.

Honour thy father and thy mother: that thy days may be long upon the land which the LORD thy God giveth thee.

Thou shalt not kill.

Thou shalt not commit adultery.

Thou shalt not steal.

Thou shalt not bear false witness against thy neighbour.

Thou shalt not covet thy neighbour's house, thou shalt not covet thy neighbour's wife, nor his manservant, nor his maidservant, nor his ox, nor his ass, nor any thing that is thy neighbour's.

And the LORD said unto Moses, Hew thee two tables of stone like unto the first: and I will write upon these tables the words that were in the first tables, which thou brakest. . . . And he hewed two tables of stone like unto the first; and Moses rose up early in the morning, and went up unto mount Sinai, as the LORD had commanded him, and took in his hand the two tables of stone. And the LORD descended in the cloud, and stood with him there, and proclaimed the name of the LORD. . . .

And he said, Behold, I make a covenant: before all thy people I will do marvels, such as have not been done in all the earth, nor in any nation: and all the people among which thou art shall see the work of the LORD: for it is a terrible thing that I will do with thee. . . .

And it came to pass, when Moses came down from Mount Sinai with the two tables of testimony in Moses' hand, when he came down from the mount, that Moses wist not that the skin of his face shone while he talked with him (Exodus 19:1, 18, 20; 20:1–17; 34:1, 4, 5, 10, 29).

> *The Bible is a page torn out of the great*
> *volume of life; torn by the hand of God and*
> *annotated by His Spirit.*
> JOSEPH PARKER

At the Mountain of Moses

Werner Keller

At Sinai something happened that is unique in the history of mankind. Here lie both the roots and the greatness of a faith without precedent or prototype which was strong enough to affect the entire globe.

Moses, this child of a world which believed in a host of deities and in gods of all shapes and forms, proclaimed his faith in one God alone. Moses was the prophet of monotheism; that is the true greatness of this incomprehensible miracle of Sinai. Moses—this unknown son and grandson of desert nomads, brought up in a foreign land—"went down unto the people and spake unto them." Nomads in their goat's-hair tents, camping in the desert under the open sky, were the first to hear this astounding message, to accept it, and to transmit it. First of all, for thirty-nine years, in the solitude of the desert, by gurgling springs, beside the still waters of shady oases, and facing the biting wind which sweeps across the sullen landscape, as they fed their sheep, their goats, and their donkeys, they spoke among themselves of the one great God Yhwh.

So begins the wonderful story of this world-embracing faith. Simple shepherds, inured to hardship, carried the great new idea, the new faith, to their homeland, whence the message was one day to go out into the whole world and to all the peoples of the earth. The great nations and mighty empires of these far off days have long since disappeared into the dark recesses of the past. But the descendants of those shepherds who were the first to pledge their faith in a sole omnipotent God are still alive today.

"I am the Lord thy God. . . . Thou shalt have no other gods before me." That was a word heard for the first time since men inhabited this planet. There was no pattern for this faith, little hint of it from other nations.

We can make this assertion with confidence, thanks to archaeological discoveries in Egypt, the land in which Moses grew up and received his education, as well as in other lands of the ancient East. Both the sun worship of Akhnaton and the appearance in Mesopotamia of a blending of many deities into one god, Ninurta, god of war, are but vague preludes to monotheism. In all these conceptions what is lacking is the concentrated power and redemptive moral purpose that are rooted in the Ten Commandments, which Moses brought down from the lonely heights of Mt. Sinai into the hearts and minds of men.

It is only among the people of Israel out of the whole of the Fertile Crescent that there is this awakening of the new idea of God in all its clarity and purity, untainted by magic, free from a variegated and grotesque imagery, and conceived as something other than a materialistic preparation for perpetuating the self beyond the grave. Without precedent and prototype likewise is the clear imperative of the Ten Commandments. The Israelites are bidden not to sin because they are under the obedience of Yahweh!

Pictured at right is Moses with the Tablets of the Law by Rembrandt van Rijn. After God had written the Commandments on the stone tablet, Moses went back to the people, who were worshiping a golden calf. Moses was so angry and frustrated that he threw the tablets to the ground and smashed them.

THE DEATH OF MOSES

Flavius Josephus

When Moses had spoken thus at the end of his life, and had foretold what would befall to every one of their tribes afterward, with the addition of a blessing to them, the multitude fell into tears, insomuch that even the women, by beating their breasts, made manifest the deep concern they had when he was about to die. The children also lamented still more, as not able to contain their grief; and thereby declared, that even at their age they were sensible of his virtue and mighty deeds; and truly there seemed to be a strife betwixt the young and the old, who should most grieve for him. The old grieved because they knew what a careful protector they were to be deprived of, and so lamented their future state, but the young grieved, not only for that, but also because it so happened that they were to be left by him before they had well tasted of his virtue.

Now one may make a guess at the excess of this sorrow and lamentation of the multitude, from what happened to the legislator himself; for although he was always persuaded that he ought not to be cast down at the approach of death, since the undergoing it was agreeable to the will of God and the law of nature, yet what the people did so overbore him, that he wept himself. Now as he went thence to the place where he was to vanish out of their sight, they all followed after him weeping; but Moses beckoned with his hand to those that were remote from him, and bade them stay behind in quiet, while he exhorted those that were near to him that they would not render his departure so lamentable. Whereupon they thought they ought to grant him that favour, to let him depart according as he himself desired; so they restrained themselves, though weeping still towards one another. All those who accompanied him were the senate, and Eleazar the high priest, and Joshua their commander.

Now as soon as they were come to the mountain called *Abarim*, (which is a very high mountain, situated over against Jericho, and one that affords, to such as are upon it, a prospect of the greatest part of the excellent land of Canaan), he dismissed the senate; and as he was going to embrace Eleazar and Joshua, and was still discoursing with them, a cloud stood over him on the sudden, and he disappeared in a certain valley, although he wrote in the holy books that he died, which was done out of fear, lest they should venture to say that, because of his extraordinary virtue, he went to God.

Now Moses lived in all one hundred and twenty years; a third part of which time, abating one month, he was the people's ruler; and he died on the last month of the year, which is called by the Macedonians *Dystrus*, but by us *Adar*, on the first day of the month. He was one that exceeded all men that ever were in understanding, and made the best use of what that understanding suggested to him. He had a very graceful way of speaking and addressing himself to the multitude; and as to his other qualifications, he had such a full command of his passions, as if he hardly had any such in his soul, and only knew them by their names, as rather perceiving them in other men than in himself. . . . So the people mourned for him thirty days: nor did ever any grief so deeply affect the Hebrews as did this upon the death of Moses: nor were those that had experienced his conduct the only persons that desired him, but those also that perused the laws he left behind him had a strong desire after him, and by them gathered the extraordinary virtue he was master of. And this shall suffice for the declaration of the manner of the death of Moses.

Pictured above is Michelangelo's statue of Moses. The artistic tradition of depicting Moses with horns arose from the misunderstanding of the Hebrew verb qaran (Exodus 34:29), which was translated as the noun "horn" instead of the verb "to shine."

Pictured above, the cuneiform writing can clearly be seen on the obelisk at the tomb of Ramses II, who is thought to have been the Pharaoh at the time of the Exodus.

ANCIENT METHODS
OF RECORDING THE WORD

Cuneiform

Cuneiform is the earliest and once most wide-spread method of writing in the areas around the Fertile Crescent. It appears to be a form of decoration depicting daily life upon stone tablets and huge rocks; and for centuries, scholars believed cuneiform was just that: decoration. It wasn't until the middle of the nineteenth century that researchers finally attempted to decipher cuneiform script and reconstruct the languages of Mesopotamia.

Sir Henry Rawlinson, a British historian, is credited with major contributions toward the unlocking of the cuneiform languages. Rawlinson became obsessed with what is known as the Rock of Behistun, a monument to Darius I, ruler of the Persian Empire from 521 to 486 B.C. The face of the rock features heroic scenes as well as cuneiform and is on a four-thousand-foot-high peak in the Zagros Mountains. The area of the cuneiform measures about sixty feet by twenty-two feet and represents three ancient languages. Rawlinson painstakingly copied the markings before beginning the translation, which he finished in 1850.

Papyrus and Parchment

Papyrus was made from the long split stems of a plant which in the Bible was called the bulrush. This is the plant that harbored the young Moses and grows profusely in the Egyptian delta. In the making of papyrus, strips are placed parallel in water with a second layer on top at right angles to the first. As the water evaporates, weight is applied and the two layers become fused together, creating a fabric-like material. Papyrus was brought to the area around the Mediterranean from the Phoenician city of Byblos. The Greek word *byblos* originally meant "papyrus." It then came to mean "books" and eventually meant "the Bible."

The word *parchment* originated in Pergamum, a city in Asia Minor whose library rivaled that of Alexandria. Parchment was originally made from sheep or calfskin. The skin was wet and then stretched thin and allowed to dry. Parchment was more durable than papyrus and soon became the most widespread material in use before man learned to make rag paper.

Pictured above is the Rosetta Stone, discovered in 1798 at Rosetta (Rashid), near the westernmost mouth of the Nile River by one of Napoleon's officers. The stone is inscribed with three languages: ancient Greek and two forms of Egyptian, the older hieroglyphic script and a later, simplified Egyptian. By reading the Greek, linguists deciphered the two ancient Egyptian hieroglyphics. The Rosetta Stone, thus, provided the clues to unlocking all of the ancient Egyptian texts and thus to the history of the Old Testament.

THE
HISTORY

The kingdom of Israel under King Solomon
had grown so mighty, so wealthy, and so
renowned far and wide that the Queen of
Sheba came with her entourage to pay
homage to the king. This painting by artist
James J. Tissot is entitled The Queen of
Sheba Visits Solomon.

JOSHUA

The Book of Joshua is the first of the Bible's twelve books of history, but its importance lies in the fact that it is the bridge between the Pentateuch (the writings of Moses) and the remainder of Scripture. Although it cannot be proven, Jewish tradition assigns the authorship of this book to Joshua.

We first meet Joshua in the Book of Exodus. Only a few days after crossing the Red Sea in their flight from Egypt, the Israelites were attacked by the Amalekites. Moses "said unto Joshua, Choose us out men, and go out, fight with Amalek" (Exodus 17:9).

Joshua's original name was *Hoshea*, meaning "salvation" (Numbers 13:8), but Moses changed it to *Yehoshua* (Numbers 13:16), meaning "Yahweh is Salvation." Joshua is also called Yeshua, a shortened form of Yehoshua, the Hebrew equivalent of the Greek name *Iesous* (Jesus). Joshua's name symbolizes that although he is the leader of the Israelite nation during the conquest, the LORD is the conqueror. In Joshua's first battle against the Amalekites, it was not the army's might that prevailed, but the might of God: "And it came to pass, when Moses held up his hand, that Israel prevailed: and when he let down his hand, Amalek prevailed. But Moses' hands were heavy; and they took a stone, and put it under him, and he sat thereon; and Aaron and Hur stayed up his hands, the one on the one side, and the other on the other side; and his hands were steady until the going down of the sun" (Exodus 17:11, 12).

As Moses approached death, God, in a tender moment, named his successor: "And the LORD said unto Moses, Behold, thy days approach that thou must die: call Joshua, and present yourselves in the tabernacle of the congregation, that I may give him a charge. And Moses and Joshua went, and presented themselves in the tabernacle of the congregation. And he gave Joshua the son of Nun a charge, and said, Be strong and of a good courage: for thou shalt bring the children of Israel into the land which I sware unto them: and I will be with thee" (Deuteronomy 31:14, 23).

Pictured at left is a painting by the French artist James Tissot depicting the Israelites marching around the walled city of Jericho.

THE BATTLE OF JERICHO

Francis A. Schaeffer

First, the Israelites had to defeat Jericho. Through archaeological digs we have a better idea of what Jericho was like than those who read the Bible in years past. Jericho was not a big city; it was only about seven acres in its entirety. What it really was was a fortress—a very strong fortress prepared to resist siege.

Joshua did not take the city merely by a clever, human military tactic. The strategy was the Lord's: "Now Jericho was straitly shut up because of the children of Israel: none went out, and none came in. And the Lord said unto Joshua, See, I have given into thine hand Jericho, and the king thereof, and the mighty men of valour" (Joshua 6:1, 2). . . .

The people were to march for six days around the city, going around it once each day with the priests leading the way. On the seventh day everyone was to march around the city seven times. Then the priests were to blow the rams' horns and the people were to cry out. When this was done, God said, the walls of the city would fall down flat and everyone could ascend up "straight before him."

Since Jericho was a small city, as was normal for the walled cities of that time, the Israelite army was large enough to completely encircle it. So by the time the first troops had marched around the walls, the last troops would just be starting. On the seventh day when the army cried out and the walls fell, all that the soldiers would have to do is march straight ahead to the center of the city and thus capture it from all sides at once.

"You won't even have to scale the walls," God said. "Every fighting man will be able to draw his sword and march straight forward. You will take the whole city with one blow."

Joshua's obedience revealed Joshua's faith. . . . Because of the promise of God, because of his experience over the past forty years, Joshua expected the walls to fall. So "Joshua said unto the people, Shout; for the Lord hath given you the city." They had marched for six days in complete silence, but now they were to shout. When the fighting men did shout, the walls fell down and the men marched in.

Was this a direct act of divine intervention? Or did God simply use a principle of vibration, the principle which explains why an opera singer can break a glass by hitting the right note? We do not know, because God has not told us, but it does not matter which is the case. This was God's strategy, and there was a complete miracle in what occurred. God had made a promise, God had given the strategy, and the victory was accomplished.

And the LORD said unto Joshua, Fear them not: for I have delivered them into thine hand; there shall not a man of them stand before thee. Then spake Joshua to the LORD in the day when the LORD delivered up the Amorites before the children of Israel, and he said in the sight of Israel, Sun, stand thou still upon Gibeon; and thou, Moon, in the valley of Ajalon. And the sun stood still, and the moon stayed, until the people had avenged themselves upon their enemies. Is not this written in the book of Jasher? So the sun stood still in the midst of heaven, and hasted not to go down about a whole day. And there was no day like that before it or after it, that the LORD hearkened unto the voice of a man: for the LORD fought for Israel.

Joshua 10:8, 12–14

THE GROWTH AND ACCEPTANCE OF THE CANON

Francis A. Schaeffer

Joshua's relation to the book teaches us an important lesson about how the canon grew and was accepted. Joshua knew Moses, the writer of the Pentateuch, personally. Joshua knew his strengths and weaknesses as a man; he knew that Moses was a sinner, that Moses made mistakes, that Moses was just a man. Nonetheless, immediately after Moses' death Joshua accepted the Pentateuch as more than the writing of Moses. He accepted it as the writing of God. Two or three hundred years were not required for the book to become sacred. As far as Joshua was concerned the Pentateuch was the canon, and the canon was the Word of God. The biblical view of the growth and acceptance of the canon is as simple as this: When it was given, God's people understood what it was. Right away it had authority.

This is why the book of Joshua is so crucial. It stands as the bridge between the Pentateuch and the post-Pentateuchal period and provides the key for understanding some important relationships between various parts of the whole Scripture.

The fact that Joshua's generation accepted the Pentateuch as authoritative is more than a mere breath of fresh air in the heavy smog which surrounds present scholarly discussion. To the Israelites, the canon was not just academic, not merely theological, but practical. Joshua and the people had a continuity of authority as they moved through history. The book was to be their environment, their mentality.

At the time of Moses, they had the authority of both Moses and the law God had commanded Moses to write. When they woke up the morning after Moses died and when they entered the promised land, they were not left in a vacuum. To use another image, because of the continuity provided by the book, there was no fracture in the authority.

In the practical problems of life, they had an objective standard of judgment which stood in an unbroken flow. . . .

In the book of Joshua, we watch the canon grow even more. Joshua 5:1 contains the phrase *until we were passed over.* The person who wrote the narrative was there! (This reminds us of the "we" passages in Acts.) Joshua 5:6 has the words *which the LORD sware unto their fathers that He would give us, a land that floweth with milk and honey.* Again the writer was present at these events. When the generation was finished, the book of Joshua, a continuation of the canon, flowed on; and it was a first-person situation.

Joshua 24:26 tells us who this person was: "And Joshua wrote these words in the book of the law." How did the canon grow? Moses wrote, and Moses died. Joshua continued to write, and the canon continued to grow. Incidentally, as a quick parenthesis, it is quite clear that the Bible always accepts Joshua as a historic character. Nehemiah 8:17 illustrates this when it says that the children of Israel had not kept the feast of booths since the days of Joshua the son of Nun.

As Joshua faced his task, then, he had with him this first great changeless factor, the written book. It provided a continuity of authority, but it was growing and would continue to grow. It grew, but it was not discontinuous. Joshua, as he led the people, had an objective standard by which to judge everything else, and the standard was so clear that God expected the ordinary people to understand it when it was periodically read to them.

> *All things desirable to men are contained in the Bible.*
> ABRAHAM LINCOLN

JUDGES

Now therefore fear the LORD, and serve Him in sincerity and in truth: and put away the gods which your fathers served on the other side of the flood, and in Egypt; and serve ye the LORD. And if it seem evil unto you to serve the LORD, choose you this day whom ye will serve; whether the gods which your fathers served that were on the other side of the flood, or the gods of the Amorites, in whose land ye dwell: but as for me and my house, we will serve the LORD.

And the people answered and said, God forbid that we should forsake the LORD, to serve other gods; For the LORD our God, He it is that brought us up and our fathers out of the land of Egypt, from the house of bondage, and which did those great signs in our sight, and preserved us in all the way wherein we went. . . . And the people said unto Joshua . . . we will serve the LORD. So Joshua made a covenant with the people that day, and . . . wrote these words in the book of the law of God.
Joshua 24:14–17, 21, 25, 26

T he Book of Judges follows Joshua and stands in stark contrast to it. Whereas Joshua is the story of complete obedience to God and His laws, the Book of Judges tells of rejection and abandonment of God's law.

The author of Judges is anonymous, but Jewish tradition attributes the authorship to Samuel.

In dating the book, it is clear that it was written after the Ark was removed from Shiloh. The phrase "In those days there was no king in Israel" (17:6, 18:1, 19:1, 21:25) indicates that Judges was written after the beginning of Saul's reign (1043 B.C.) but before the divided kingdom. In Judges 1:21, "the Jebusites dwell with the children of Benjamin in Jerusalem unto this day" indicates that it was written before 1004 B.C. when David captured Jerusalem and dispossessed the Jebusites.

Judges describes a 350-year "dark age" of Israel, following Joshua's death. Joshua had reiterated to the people that they were to keep, read, and meditate upon the Law, yet it seems that with the passing of that generation, "there arose another generation after them, which knew not the LORD, nor yet the works which He had done for Israel" (2:10).

The rest of the Book of Judges describes several cycles which include "rebellion, retribution, repentance, restoration, and rest." The final result at the end of the Book of Judges, however, is one of the worst periods of degradation in the whole Bible. Just as the author of Judges began his work with the clue to the cycle of sin when he said the people "did evil in the sight of the LORD," the author closes the book with the key to the period: "every man did that which was right in his own eyes." These people—whose ancestors had seen Moses come down from the mountain, glowing from being in the presence of the LORD, and whose grandparents had marched around the city of Jericho and seen the walls tumble—had amazingly forsaken the moral code and laws of God and did only what seemed to be pleasurable to themselves.

Pictured at left is a portion of the Citadel in Jerusalem.

RUTH

Goethe called the Book of Ruth the most beautiful "little whole" of the Hebrew Bible. The book's origin and basis have remained elusive. Jewish tradition attributes the authorship to Samuel, but this is probably not the case since David appears in the Book of Ruth, and Samuel died before David's coronation. It is likely that Ruth was written during David's reign. Whatever its source, the book has universal and timeless appeal as the story of life in a typical town. It includes one of the loveliest passages of loyalty found anywhere, which, in the King James Version, stands as one of the most beautiful works of literature:

> And Naomi said unto her two daughters-in-law, Go, return each to her mother's house: the LORD deal kindly with you, as ye have dealt with the dead, and with me. The LORD grant you that ye may find rest, each of you in the house of her husband.
>
> Then she kissed them; and they lifted up their voice, and wept. And they said unto her, Surely we will return with thee unto thy people.
>
> And Naomi said, Turn again, my daughters: why will ye go with me? are there yet any more sons in my womb, that they may be your husbands? Turn again, my daughters, go your way; for I am too old to have an husband. If I should say, I have hope, if I should have an husband also tonight, and should also bear sons; Would ye tarry for them till they were grown? would ye stay for them from having husbands? nay, my daughters; for it grieveth me much for your sakes that the hand of the LORD is gone out against me.
>
> And they lifted up their voice, and wept again: and Orpah kissed her mother-in-law; but Ruth clave unto her.
>
> And she said, Behold, thy sister-in-law is gone back unto her people, and unto her gods: return thou after thy sister-in-law.
>
> And Ruth said, Intreat me not to leave thee, or to return from following after thee: for whither thou goest, I will go; and where thou lodgest, I will lodge: thy people shall be my people, and thy God my God (1:8–16).

Pictured at right is a painting of Ruth gleaning wheat in the field of Boaz. The painting is by the French artist James J. Tissot.

THE BOOKS OF SAMUEL

The LORD called Samuel . . . And he ran unto Eli, and said, Here am I; for thou calledst me. And he said, I called not; lie down again. And he went and lay down. . . .

And the LORD called Samuel again the third time. And he arose and went to Eli, and said, Here am I; for thou didst call me. And Eli perceived that the LORD had called the child. Therefore Eli said unto Samuel, Go, lie down: and it shall be, if He call thee, that thou shalt say, Speak, LORD; for thy servant heareth.

So Samuel went and lay down in his place. And the LORD came, and stood, and called as at other times, Samuel, Samuel. Then Samuel answered, Speak; for thy servant heareth.

1 Samuel 3:4, 5, 8–10

The first and second Books of Samuel describe the foundation and history of the Israelite monarchy. They tell the story of Samuel, the last judge and first prophet of Israel; of Saul, the first king of Israel; and finally of David, the shepherd boy who was anointed as successor to Saul.

The two Books of Samuel, which exist as one book in the Hebrew text, were first divided into two books in the Greek Septuagint. Jewish tradition ascribes the authorship to Samuel. Although his story dominates the text of the books and he could have written part of 1 Samuel, his death in 1 Samuel 25:1 makes it clear that Samuel did not write all of both Books of Samuel.

First Chronicles 29:29 refers to "the book of Samuel the Seer," "the book of Nathan the Prophet," and "the book of Gad the seer." All three men evidently contributed to these two books. Because of the smooth transitions between the sections and the cohesiveness of the books, some scholars believe a single compiler, possibly a member of the prophetic school, used these chronicles to put together Samuel.

In 1 Samuel, we are given one of the primary Old Testament portrayals of the Person of Christ in David. David, like Jesus, was born in Bethlehem, was a shepherd, and ruled as king of Israel. As the anointed king, he is the forerunner of the messianic King. The Psalms of David are borne out of years of rejection and danger, specifically Psalm 22. The New Testament specifically calls Christ the "seed of David according to the flesh" (Romans 1:3) and "the Root and the Offspring of David" (Revelation 22:16).

In the book of 2 Samuel, we read of David's reign over Judah and then over the entire nation of Israel. But there are also the narratives of adultery and murder, and the consequences of those sins, not only upon his family, but upon the entire nation of Israel. In fact, 2 Samuel can be divided into three distinct divisions: the triumphs of David (chapters 1–10), the transgressions of David (11), and the troubles of David (12–24). The remaining chapters show how closely the affairs of the people are tied to the spiritual and moral condition of the king.

The image pictured at right is a page from an illuminated manuscript depicting Samuel being sent by God to Bethlehem; six elders of Bethlehem greeting Samuel at the gate; and Samuel demanding to see David after rejecting the other sons of Jesse.

THE BOOKS
OF THE KINGS

L ike the Books of Samuel, the two Books of Kings were originally one in the Hebrew Bible and were divided in the
Septuagint. Some scholars speculate that the division
occurred for a very practical reason. The Septuagint was written in
Greek, a language that requires more space than Hebrew; this would
have resulted in a longer scroll than the original Hebrew.

The account of the Kings begins with the life of Solomon. Under
his reign, Israel rises to her zenith in size and glory. Solomon initiates a
building program, which includes the construction of the magnificent
Temple in Jerusalem, that brings him fame throughout the known
world. In spite of his earlier promise and wish for wisdom, Solomon in
his later years seems to turn toward a search for fame and worldly
respect and away from the ways of God. As a result, the king with the
divided heart leaves behind a divided kingdom.

The remainder of 1 Kings traces twin histories of two kings and two
kingdoms, both filled with disobedient people who are indifferent to,
and for the most part ignorant of, the Laws of God and Moses.
Nineteen consecutive ungodly kings rule Israel, leading to its captivity
by Assyria. Judah occasionally has a king that institutes reform; but by
550 B.C., the people of Judah are also marched off to Babylon.

The authorship of Kings is unknown, although Jewish tradition suggests the prophet Jeremiah. The author was most
certainly a prophet and historian, and the writing
style is similar to that in Jeremiah. If the books were
not written by Jeremiah himself (c. 646 to 570
B.C.), they were certainly written by his contemporary. The omission of Jeremiah's ministry in the
narrative of King Josiah and his successors may
indicate that Jeremiah himself was the recorder of
the events. The last two chapters, however, were
probably added to the book after the Babylonian
captivity and not written by Jeremiah since he fled
to Egypt, not Babylon.

*Pictured below is a relief
depicting the siege of Israel.*

THE BOOKS
OF THE CHRONICLER

In that night did God appear unto Solomon, and said unto him, Ask what I shall give thee.

And Solomon said unto God, Thou hast shewed great mercy unto David my father, and hast made me to reign in his stead. Now, O LORD God, let Thy promise unto David my father be established: for Thou hast made me king over a people like the dust of the earth in multitude. Give me now wisdom and knowledge, that I may go out and come in before this people: for who can judge this Thy people, that is so great?

And God said to Solomon, Because this was in thine heart, and thou hast not asked riches, wealth, or honour, nor the life of thine enemies, neither yet hast asked long life; but hast asked wisdom and knowledge for thyself, that thou mayest judge my people, over whom I have made thee king: Wisdom and knowledge is granted unto thee; and I will give thee riches, and wealth, and honour, such as none of the kings have had that have been before thee, neither shall there any after thee have the like.

2 Chronicles 1:7–12

The Books of Samuel and Kings provided a major source for the Books of Chronicles; but Chronicles contains several unique passages. Whereas Samuel and Kings provide a political history of Israel and Judah, the Chronicles present the spiritual history.

As were the Books of Samuel and Kings, the two Books of Chronicles were one in the original Hebrew. Chronicles was divided into two parts in the Greek translation of the Hebrew Bible known as the Septuagint. It was entitled "Of Things Omitted," referring to that which was omitted from Samuel and Kings. The title *Chronicles* was given the books by Jerome in his Latin Vulgate Bible.

The author of the Chronicles is unknown and is often referred to as "the Chronicler." A traditional view named Ezra as author, but it cannot even be said with certainty that the Chronicles are the work of a single author. In fact, scholars cannot pin down a date of composition for the Chronicles. The books were addressed to the remnant who returned to Israel in 457 B.C.; and the books could have been completed sometime between 450 and 430 B.C.

In the Chronicles, we see a different side of David's life. The writer of the Chronicles, called "the Chronicler," was writing later than the author of Samuel and Kings. Some scholars believe he made use of the information in Samuel and Kings and, in some cases, repeated much of these earlier books. Yet the Chronicler omitted much from the earlier books. David's struggles with Saul, his reign in Hebron, his various wives, and Absalom's rebellion are all omitted. The writer also omits the event that colored the rest of David's life: his adultery with Bathsheba.

The Chronicles emphasize God's grace, an encouragement to the Jews who had just returned from captivity. And the Chronicler added events not found in Samuel, such as David's preparations for the Temple. The books' message can be summed up in 2 Chronicles 7:14: "If my people, which are called by my name, shall humble themselves, and pray, and seek my face, and turn from their wicked ways; then will I hear from heaven, and will forgive their sin, and will heal their land."

Elijah and Elisha

Elijah and Elisha were prophets in the ninth century B.C. in the northern kingdom, but we know little else personal about them. Elijah's name translates as "Yah[weh] is my God." He came from Israel and prophesied during the reigns of Ahab, Ahaziah, and Jehoram (873 to 843 B.C.), kings of the northern kingdom of Israel. No Book of Elijah appears in the Bible; but he dominates the Books of Kings as God's answer to the evil King Ahab.

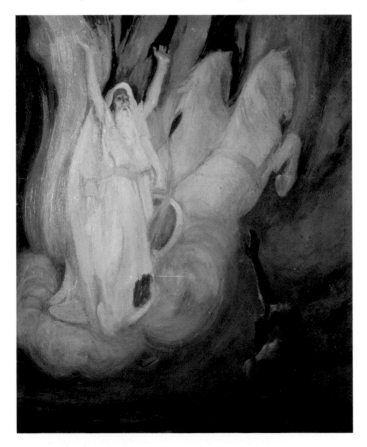

The painting at right is an artistic rendering of Elijah returning the widow's son to his mother after the prophet brought the child back to life. The work was created by English painter Ford Madox Brown in the mid-eighteenth century.

The painting at left depicts Elijah ascending into heaven in a chariot of fire with his successor, Elisha, looking on. The work is by James J. Tissot, a French artist painting in the late nineteenth century.

In 1 Kings 17 through 19, Elijah foretells of a devastating drought. When the drought comes, God protects Elijah from its effects and also from the angry king. Elijah then challenges the king and his prophets to a contest to determine whose God will end the drought. Yahweh's consumption of the bull offered to Him proves that He alone is God and that the rain that falls is therefore from Him and not from the pagan god Baal. Elijah is eventually taken up to heaven in 2 Kings 2:11. Jewish tradition remembers him as a prophet of the coming Messiah; at the Passover table, a place is set for Elijah in case he returns to announce the beginning of the age of the Messiah.

Elisha's name means "God has granted salvation." The son of Shaphat, he was a native of Abel-Meholah in the northern kingdom of Israel and lived and prophesied during the reigns of Jehoram, Jehu, Jehoahaz, and Joash. Told in 2 Kings, Elisha's story appears mostly in two forms. There are lengthy narratives in which the prophet, sometimes with his servant Gehazi, is involved with great leaders of the age. Elisha advises the kings of Israel, Judah, and Edom in their war with Moab. He plays a role in wars between Syria and Israel, and he helps to foment the rebellion of Jehu. Elisha is a doer of miracles, a true prophet of God and the successor of Elijah, who casts his mantle upon Elisha as a symbolic proffering of his position as prophet.

EZRA

In 586 B.C., the Babylonians captured Jerusalem and the invaders looted the Temple, burning it to the ground; ancient scrolls and the sacred Ark were lost forever. Hundreds of Jews were taken to Babylon, exiled from their homeland. The exiled Jews began to meet in small groups for worship and instruction in their religion. According to tradition, when the Jewish captives finally returned to their homeland in Palestine after seventy years of exile, it was Ezra who collected the writings that make up the Old Testament, writings which had been miraculously preserved through the long years of exile.

The Books of Ezra and Nehemiah were originally one book because Chronicles, Ezra, and Nehemiah were viewed as one continuous history. The Septuagint calls Ezra-Nehemiah, Second Esdras. (First Esdras is the name of an apocryphal Book of Esdras.) Most scholars believe the author, or at least the editor, of Chronicles was Ezra.

According to the book that bears his name, Ezra was a "priest, the scribe, even a scribe of the words of the commandments of the LORD, and of his statutes to Israel" (7:11). Ezra had probably grown up in Babylon, in exile, but he received from Persian King Artaxerxes the right to instruct Jews on the law in religious matters. Ezra studied, practiced, and taught the law of the Lord as an educated scribe and had access to the library of Nehemiah. Some scholars think Ezra composed Nehemiah as well by using Nehemiah's personal diary.

The Book of Ezra describes two returns to Jerusalem: the first led by Zerubbabel to rebuild the Temple and the second under the leadership of Ezra to rebuild the spiritual life of the people. Fifteen hundred families of Jews accompanied Ezra in approximately 458 B.C., and the Book of Ezra describes their efforts to rebuild the Temple—a task frustrated by their enemies. Ezra brings with him a group of exiles including priests and Levites, but he is disappointed to find that the remnant of Jews in Jerusalem has intermarried with neighboring nations, and he orders the Jews to repudiate their foreign spouses.

Ezra wrote his book between 457 B.C. and 444 B.C. (Nehemiah's arrival in Jerusalem). During the period covered by the Book of Ezra, Confucius is teaching in China and Socrates in Greece.

Then were assembled unto me every one that trembled at the words of the God of Israel, because of the transgression of those that had been carried away; and I sat astonied until the evening sacrifice.

And at the evening sacrifice I arose up from my heaviness; and having rent my garment and my mantle, I fell upon my knees, and spread out my hands unto the Lord my God, And said, O my God, I am ashamed and blush to lift up my face to Thee, my God: for our iniquities are increased over our head, and our trespass is grown up unto the heavens. . . . And now for a little space grace hath been shown from the Lord our God, to leave us a remnant to escape, and to give us a nail in His holy place, that our God may lighten our eyes, and give us a little reviving in our bondage.

Ezra 9:4–6, 8

Pictured at right is an illustration from the Codex Amiatinus, *a biblical manuscript that dates from the early eighth century. In the illustration, Ezra is shown writing his book.*

ESTHER

With a title taken from the name of its heroine, the Book of Esther describes unsuccessful attempts to kill the Jews living in the Persian Empire during the reign of a certain Ahasuerus, probably King Xerxes, from 486 to 485 B.C. Displaying great courage and shrewdness, Esther, with the help of her cousin Mordecai, saves her people.

Although the theme of the book is God's protection of His people, His name does not appear once. A plot by the king's courtier, Haman, endangers the Jews; and Esther's courage, along with the counsel of Mordecai, brings deliverance of her people. Today, the annual Feast of Purim still reminds the Jews of God's faithfulness on behalf of His people.

Neither the date nor the author of the Book of Esther has been agreed upon by scholars, as there are no clear historical allusions to pin it down precisely. The book concerns itself with the time of King Ahasuerus's reign in Persia from 486 to 464 B.C. Esther was written for the many Jews who did not return to Judah. Some could not get back; others stayed out of disobedience. Esther clearly illustrated that God continued to care for His people no matter where they were.

NEHEMIAH

N ehemiah came from Susa in Persia to rebuild the walls of Jerusalem in about 444 B.C. He had been the cupbearer, a high office with influence, at the court of the Persian King Artaxerxes. Nehemiah heard that the city of Jerusalem was in ruins and his people were trying, unsuccessfully, to rebuild the Temple; he petitioned the king for permission to go to Jerusalem to help. The king not only granted his request, but made him governor of Judah.

Accompanied by an escort of soldiers, Nehemiah went to the city, and one of his first acts was to inspect the city's walls and then organize the Jews to rebuild them. Nehemiah governed Judah for twelve years before returning to the royal court in Persia. After a few years' absence, however, he returned to Jerusalem and was shocked by what he saw. He took forceful action to bring the city back under the Law.

Most scholars believe that much of this book came from Nehemiah's personal memoirs. Some scholars believe that Nehemiah composed some portions and compiled the rest. Other scholars believe that Ezra wrote some of the passages and compiled the rest using Nehemiah's diary. Ezra brought spiritual revival to the Israelites at the return to Jerusalem, and Nehemiah brought physical restoration. Both were necessary; for without a wall, Jerusalem was really not a city at all.

In Nehemiah, we glimpse the excitement of the reading of the Book of the Law, the rejection of which had unleashed the cycles of sin and redemption ending in the exile. "And they spake unto Ezra the scribe to bring the book of the law of Moses, which the LORD had commanded to Israel. . . . And he read therein . . . before the water gate from the morning until midday, before the men and the women, and those that could understand; and the ears of all the people were attentive unto the book of the law. And Ezra opened the book in the sight of all the people; (for he was above all the people;) and when he opened it, all the people stood up: And Ezra blessed the LORD, the great God. And all the people answered, Amen, Amen" (8:1b, 3, 5, 6). The Book of Nehemiah marks the end of the historical account in the Old Testament, about four hundred years before the birth of the promised Messiah.

Pictured above left is a Hebrew manuscript of the Book of Esther.

Pictured at left is a page from a decorated Hebrew scroll of the Book of Esther that dates from the 1800s. The illumination on the scroll would never have been used on the Torah.

THE
POETRY

JOB

The three Books of Proverbs, Job, and Ecclesiastes have been called "wisdom literature." Wisdom literature professed the belief in a universal truth and held the individual accountable for his actions. The writers of wisdom literature believed that one's intellect could cope with and overcome every eventuality. But they also believed that human intellect was limited, and prophets and psalmists alike looked to God for the ultimate answers. The ultimate goal was to discover what would enable one to live long and live well—a goal that requires a reliable and orderly cosmos from which to draw lessons with predictable outcomes.

The Book of Job is an extended discussion on the meaning of human suffering, and literary critics unanimously consider it a masterpiece worthy of inclusion among the classics of world literature. It is perhaps the oldest book of the Bible; its theme is ancient and ongoing.

There are no hints to indicate the date of the writing of Job nor its author. The story, however, is set in the patriarchal period, the period of Abraham, Isaac, and Jacob. Job's wealth is measured in livestock (1:3) rather than in gold and silver; he is the priest of his family and offers sacrifices. There are no references to Israel, the Exodus, or to Abraham's time. And Job used the characteristic patriarchal name for God, *Shaddai* ("the Almighty") thirty-one times, although the term is found only seventeen times in the rest of the Old Testament.

The book begins with a debate between God and Satan, moves to three debates between Job and his friends, and ends with God's summary of Job's problems. Although Job loses everything except his life, he acknowledges the sovereignty of God, and his wealth is restored and multiplied. Throughout his trials, Job remains steadfast in his faith and acknowledges his need for a Redeemer.

"Oh that my words were now written! oh that they were printed in a book! That they were graven with an iron pen and lead in the rock for ever. For I know that my redeemer liveth, and that He shall stand at the latter day upon the earth: And though after my skin worms destroy this body, yet in my flesh shall I see God: Whom I shall see for myself, and mine eyes shall behold, and not another" (19:23–27).

Then the LORD answered Job out of the whirlwind, and said, Who is this that darkeneth counsel by words without knowledge? Gird up now thy loins like a man; for I will demand of thee, and answer thou me. Where wast thou when I laid the foundations of the earth? declare, if thou hast understanding. . . .

Then Job answered the LORD, and said, I know that Thou canst do every thing, and that no thought can be withholden from Thee. Who is he that hideth counsel without knowledge? therefore have I uttered that I understood not; things too wonderful for me, which I knew not. Hear, I beseech Thee, and I will speak: I will demand of Thee, and declare Thou unto me. I have heard of Thee by the hearing of the ear: but now mine eye seeth Thee. Wherefore I abhor myself, and repent in dust and ashes.

Job 38:1–4; 42:1–6

Pictured at right is just one of the many artistic renderings that the story of Job has evoked. In this painting by William Blake, Job is depicted before the whirlwind of God.

THE PSALMS

Certainly most people, if asked, would name the Book of Psalms as one of their most beloved of all the books of the Bible. The Bible gives superscriptions regarding the authorship of the Psalms; and although these have been challenged by some scholars, tradition and evidence uphold them. Almost half of the psalms are attributed to David. In addition, Acts 4:25 and Hebrews 4:7 attribute two additional psalms (2 and 95) to David as well. David's life as shepherd, musician, warrior, and king is reflected in these psalms. Remaining psalms are attributed to various people, including Asaph, a priest who supervised the music; the sons of Korah; and a guild of singers and composers. Two more were written by Solomon, one by Moses, one by Heman, and one by Ethan. Fifty of the Psalms are anonymous, and some scholars attribute some of these to Ezra.

When the Psalms were originally collected in a book, it was unnamed. It later came to be known as *Sepher Tehillium*, meaning a book of praises, because almost every one of the psalms contains some word of praise to God. The Septuagint uses the Greek word *Psalmoi* as its title, meaning poems sung to the accompaniment of musical instruments. It also calls the book *Psalterium*, or a collection of songs. This word is the root for the term *Psalter*. The Latin title is *Liber Psalmorum*, meaning Book of Psalms, our term today.

In Jewish and Christian tradition, the Psalter is one of the most treasured books. It is considered a school of prayer, not only because it contains prayers that can be used for personal use, but because it also teaches one to pray. The familiarity of the lament, the enthusiasm of the hymn, and the confessional character of the thanksgiving all speak to the human heart before God.

DAVID

Chaim Potok

When David learned of the death of Saul and Jonathan, he gave expression to his mourning in a dirge of moving lyric quality. "Thy beauty, O Israel, upon thy high places is slain! How have the mighty fallen! . . ." Then he gathered up his troops, their wives and children and possessions, and, no doubt with the approval of his Philistine overlord, moved to Hebron, the chief city of the tribe of Judah. There he camped, and waited.

We will never know if he actually coveted the kingship during the life of Saul; doubtlessly he did; just as doubtlessly he would have done nothing against the king to obtain it. He was a profoundly devout man and would never have raised a hand against the anointed one of YHWH. But he possessed an uncanny ability to read events, to anticipate the future, to move toward it and patiently await its coming. As he waited now in Hebron. . . .

Negotiations resumed between David and representatives of the elders of the north. At the end the elders came to Hebron and covenanted with David, "and they anointed David king over Israel."

He was thirty years old. He had reigned in Hebron over Judah seven and a half years. Now north and south were united in his person; he was king of the two lands of Judah and Israel.

He had attained kingship not through any charismatic action that might have shown him to be possessed of the spirit of the Lord but through the sordid realities of political and military power and the adroit use of diplomacy. For the many clans that dwelt in the extensive territory of Judah, charismatic leadership ended when kingship was given to David. It is not entirely certain that it came to an end as well for the tribes of the north. . . .

The land had two capitals, Hebron and Mahanaim, a politically divisive situation. The range of hills that had been the physical barrier between north and south now beckoned David into a daring move. He brought his small army northward, and in a sudden maneuver that remains unexplained despite the claim of some that they understand how it was done—a swift scaling of the walls; a surprise attack through an underground water channel—he captured the Jebusite city of Jerusalem. Archaeologists tell us that it measured around twelve acres—about 1250 feet from north to south and 400 feet from east to west. Its small houses were crowded together; its streets were narrow and crooked. What mattered most in an ancient city was not the comfort of space but the protection of walls. Jerusalem was thick-walled and perched on a mountain ridge in the shape, roughly, of a V. David permitted the surrendering Jebusites to remain in the city and brought his retinue inside. It was his city, taken with his own troops. It controlled a vital mountain road that linked the northern and southern regions of the land. He was obligated to no tribe for its capture. It was renamed the city of David. He made it the capital of the united monarchy of Judah and Israel. . . .

The ark of YHWH had remained neglected all these years in the village of Kiriath-jearim. Now David had it brought in joyous procession to Jerusalem. He himself led the procession and danced before the ark in uncontrollable ecstasy. The city of Jerusalem—his city—was raised to the rank of cultic center of the united monarchy. City, clans, ark, and kingship were now linked.

THE SWEETEST VOICE

Laurance Wieder

Most readers know the Book of Psalms in one of the many translations that have appeared since the beginning of the Common Era. . . . The Hebrew original stands before these versions like a model before an art class. Even, or especially, if the artists are all masters, no two depictions look the same. Still, the casual visitor to the studio can judge how closely, if at all, the artwork resembles the model. If unrecognizable, then the picture may be something else, but it is not a picture of "the book." This representational standard separates literary or classical from scriptural poetry.

But the original is elusive. The Hebrew text was received without vowels, is unpronounceable like the name of God. So the Masoretes, those scholars who committed the tradition to paper, made two columns: the text as received (what is read), and the same text with vowel points inserted (what is said). To speak the words is to translate, to interpret. The unpointed text poses for the rabbis, as a model, a question, a picture of the unseen and unimaginable. All agree that the it is there, but no two mouths can say the same or show the all of it. . . .

In The *Midrash on Psalms,* the rabbis teach that Moses has five books, and David has five. . . . The *Midrash* states that just as the Psalms are attributed to ten authors, so there are also ten kinds of song: glory, melody, Psalm, song, praise, prayer, blessing, thanksgiving, Hallelujah, and exultation. . . . The Sages agree on the names of the ten contributors to the Book of Psalms: Adam, Melchizedek, Abraham, Moses, David, Solomon, Asaph, and the three sons of Korah. The names of David's court musicians, who probably composed some of the Psalms, are not recorded outside the incidental appearances of their names in scripture. . . .

Though certain psalms bear the name of one of the ten authors, the book as a whole bears the name of David, king of Israel. As a parable tells us, there was a company of musicians who sought to sing a hymn to the king. The king said to them: To be sure, all of you are skilled musicians, all of you are devout, all of you are worthy of taking part in the singing of a hymn before me, yet let the hymn be sung by So-and-so only, on behalf of all of you. Why? Because his voice is sweetest.

A PSALM OF DAVID.

The LORD is my shepherd; I shall not want. He maketh me to lie down in green pastures: He leadeth me beside the still waters. He restoreth my soul: He leadeth me in the paths of righteousness for His name's sake. Yea, though I walk through the valley of the shadow of death, I will fear no evil: for Thou art with me; Thy rod and Thy staff they comfort me. Thou preparest a table before me In the presence of mine enemies: Thou anointest my head with oil; my cup runneth over. Surely goodness and mercy shall follow me all the days of my life: and I will dwell in the house of the Lord for ever.

Psalm 23

> *The incongruity of the Bible with the age of its birth, its freedom from earthly mixtures, its original, unborrowed, solitary greatness; the suddenness with which it broke forth amidst the general gloom; these, to me, are strong indications of its divine descent: I cannot reconcile them with a human origin.*
>
> WILLIAM ELLERY CHANNING

SOLOMON

Solomon was the son of King David and Bathsheba. Although not in the line of succession and born of an adulterous relationship, Solomon was, nevertheless, chosen by David as his successor. King Solomon prayed for wisdom and God granted his request; unlike his father, Solomon was able to build the Temple, which became the home for the Scriptures at least during his reign.

The king became legendary, even during his own time, for his sense of justice. The Queen of Sheba, from southwest Arabia, about where Yemen is today, came to see him. Sheba was prosperous and a symbol of wealth at the time. The Queen brought extravagant gifts and came armed with questions to test Solomon's knowledge and justice. This visit stands as a testament to Solomon's internationalism and diplomacy. His rule was marked by peace throughout his large kingdom and was sustained through his skill as a diplomat rather than the military force of his father David.

Pictured below are the ruins of the ancient city of Megiddo. The city, built by Solomon, is now being excavated. Archaeologists have uncovered ruins of huge stables, possibly those of Solomon as described in 1 Kings 10:26, 28.

"And God gave Solomon wisdom and understanding exceeding much, and largeness of heart, even as the sand that is on the sea shore. And Solomon's wisdom excelled the wisdom of . . . all the wisdom of Egypt. For he was wiser than all men . . . and his fame was in all nations round about. And he spake three thousand proverbs: and his songs were a thousand and five . . . . And there came of all people to hear the wisdom of Solomon, from all kings of the earth, which had heard of his wisdom" (1 Kings 4:29–32, 34).

Solomon is credited with writing the Book of Proverbs, a book of wisdom; Ecclesiastes, a book on the meaning of life; and Song of Solomon, a book of love. Jewish tradition asserts that he wrote Song of Solomon in his youthful years, Proverbs in his middle years, and Ecclesiastes in his later years.

PROVERBS

A good name is rather to be chosen than great riches, and loving favour rather than silver and gold. The rich and poor meet together: the Lord is the maker of them all.

A prudent man foreseeth the evil, and hideth himself: but the simple pass on, and are punished. By humility and the fear of the Lord are riches, and honour, and life. Thorns and snares are in the way of the froward: he that doth keep his soul shall be far from them.

Train up a child in the way he should go: and when he is old, he will not depart from it. The rich ruleth over the poor, and the borrower is servant to the lender.

He that soweth iniquity shall reap vanity: and the rod of his anger shall fail. He that hath a bountiful eye shall be blessed; for he giveth of his bread to the poor. Cast out the scorner, and contention shall go out; yea, strife and reproach shall cease.

Proverbs 22:1–10

Traditionally, the authorship of the Book of Proverbs is attributed to King Solomon. The Hebrew, Greek, and Latin titles all translate to mean the Proverbs of Solomon. Most scholars recognize five separate divisions in the Book of Proverbs. The first, including Proverbs 1:1 through 9:18, is identified as the Proverbs of Solomon and includes instructional essays on the nature of wisdom, the meaning of life, and the path to success. The second division includes those verses from Proverbs 10:1 through 22:16. These verses are much simpler in style than the first section and may contain proverbs assembled and used by the scribes of King Hezekiah's reign. Other scholars point to Isaiah and Micah as possibly involved in this collection. The third division includes Proverbs 22:17 through 24:22, and scholars have given this group the name "words of the wise." It consists of a compilation of thirty instructions, some of them similar to an Egyptian document of teachings dating from about 1000 B.C. Some biblical scholars believe the Egyptian collector borrowed these sayings from the Proverbs collection. The fourth collection of Proverbs, 24:23–34 is similar to the third, whereas the fifth and final collection, Proverbs 25:1 through 29:27, is clearly named as the "Proverbs of Solomon." These are the "proverbs that the officials of King Hezekiah of Judah copied."

The Book of Proverbs is, perhaps, second only to the Psalms as a beloved book of reading. The book offers its reader wisdom and shows how to cope with life, to evolve practical rules of comportment, and to develop balanced judgment, as the beginning verses make clear:

"The proverbs of Solomon the son of David, king of Israel; To know wisdom and instruction; to perceive the words of understanding; To receive the instruction of wisdom, justice, and judgment, and equity; To give subtelty to the simple, to the young man knowledge and discretion. A wise man will hear, and will increase learning; and a man of understanding shall attain unto wise counsels: To understand a proverb, and the interpretation; the words of the wise, and their dark sayings. The fear of the LORD is the beginning of knowledge: but fools despise wisdom and instruction" (Proverbs 1:1–7).

ECCLESIASTES

Ecclesiastes is one individual's conclusions about life and the world based upon experience and observation. Most scholars believe the recurring phrases and consistent level of sophistication of language point to a single author. The writer takes the persona of "the Preacher," and the book is an essay on the meaninglessness of life without God.

The author of the Book of Ecclesiastes is traditionally known as King Solomon, as the writer explains in the first verse of the book: "The words of the Preacher, the son of David, king in Jerusalem" (1:1). Since Solomon was the only son of David to reign in Jerusalem, the evidence certainly supports Solomon as author.

The Preacher looks for meaning in all of the traditional places—in pleasure, in riches, in work. But he discovers that these are all meaningless. Even man's wisdom proves meaningless at the end of life. Nothing can fill man's life but God Himself, and only through faith in God does life take on meaning and purpose. The book that began with "Vanity of vanities, saith the Preacher, vanity of vanities; all is vanity" (1:2) ends with the confirmation of life: "Fear God, and keep His commandments: for this is the whole duty of man" (12:13).

SONG OF SOLOMON

The authorship of the Song of Solomon is traditionally ascribed to King Solomon. Taken as literature, it is a lyrical poem written with emotional warmth that shares the universal language of love. It tells of the wooing and wedding of a shepherdess by King Solomon and the joys and heartaches of wedded love.

But when taken to a deeper level, the poem becomes allegorical, and the bride and bridegroom symbolic. In the Old Testament, Israel is regarded as the bride of Yahweh (Isaiah 54:5), whereas in the New Testament, the church is seen as the bride of Christ (Ephesians 5:23–25). Most theologians interpret the Song of Solomon as illustrating the former and anticipating the latter.

Pictured at right is artist Giambattista Tiepolo's depiction of the well-known scripture in which Solomon is asked to ascertain which mother is the birth mother of a baby. The king does so by commanding the baby be split in half. The real mother is willing to give up her claim rather than have her child killed.

King Solomon Builds the Temple

And it came to pass in the four hundred and eightieth year after the children of Israel were come out of the land of Egypt, in the fourth year of Solomon's reign over Israel, In the month Zif, which is the second month, that he began to build the house of the Lord. . . .

And the house, when it was in building, was built of stone made ready before it was brought thither: so that there was neither hammer nor axe nor any tool of iron heard in the house, while it was in building. . . .

So Solomon built the house, and finished it. And he built the walls of the house within with boards of cedar, both the floor of the house, and the walls of the ceiling: and he covered them on the inside with wood, and covered the floor of the house with planks of fir. . . . And the cedar of the house within was carved with knobs and open flowers: all was cedar; there was no stone seen. And the oracle he prepared in the house within, to set there the ark of the covenant of the Lord. . . .

So Solomon overlaid the house within with pure gold: and he made a partition by the chains of gold before the oracle; and he overlaid it with gold. And the whole house he overlaid with gold, until he had finished all the house: also the whole altar that was by the oracle he overlaid with gold. And within the oracle he made two cherubims of olive tree, each ten cubits high. . . .

And in the eleventh year, in the month Bul, which is the eighth month, was the house finished throughout all the parts thereof, and according to all the fashion of it. So was he seven years in building it. . . .

And they brought up the ark of the Lord, and the tabernacle of the congregation. . . . And the priests brought in the ark of the covenant of the Lord unto his place, into the oracle of the house, to the most holy place, even under the wings of the cherubims. . . . There was nothing in the ark save the two tables of stone, which Moses put there at Horeb, when the Lord made a covenant with the children of Israel, when they came out of the land of Egypt.

And it came to pass, when the priests were come out of the holy place, that the cloud filled the house of the Lord, So that the priests could not stand to minister because of the cloud: for the glory of the Lord had filled the house of the Lord.

Then spake Solomon, The Lord said that He would dwell in the thick darkness. I have surely built Thee an house to dwell in, a settled place for Thee to abide in for ever.

And Solomon stood before the altar of the Lord . . . . And he said, Lord God of Israel, there is no God like Thee, in heaven above, or on earth beneath, who keepest covenant and mercy with Thy servants that walk before Thee with all their heart . . .

And he stood, and blessed all the congregation of Israel with a loud voice, saying, Blessed be the Lord, that hath given rest unto His people Israel, according to all that He promised . . .The Lord our God be with us, as He was with our fathers: let Him not leave us, nor forsake us: That He may incline our hearts unto Him, to walk in all His ways, and to keep His commandments, and His statutes, and His judgments, which He commanded our fathers (1 Kings 6:1,7, 14-15, 18-19, 21-23, 38; 8:4, 6, 9-13,22-23, 55-58).

Pictured at right is a page from an illuminated text with Jean Fouquet's painting Building of the Temple of Jerusalem.

Aund en auū de quā
tes uertus et de quantz
biens il a este aucteur
a ceulr de sa liguee. et
combien plain de grant age il est
mort nous lauons declaire ou li

ure deuant dict. Quand salomo
son fil. auquies icelnie enfant eut
prins le roraume de son pere. et sa
assis ou siege roral. tout le peuple
solēnelmēnt faueur. comme on
seult faire a uū roy au commence

THE
MAJOR
PROPHETS

*Pictured at right is the Old City of
Jerusalem.*

THE DIVIDED KINGDOM

With the death of Solomon, about 928 B.C, no successor arose with the strong hand of David nor with the diplomacy and wisdom of Solomon, and the nation soon split into two kingdoms. The division was the manifestation of long-standing disputes. Even in David's time, the northern tribes had resented the heavy burdens of taxation and forced labor imposed on them; and during the reign of Solomon, northern tribes had rebelled in an unsuccessful attempt at independence. The north became Israel. The tribe of Judah, along with the tiny tribe of Benjamin, formed a southern kingdom known as Judah; this southern kingdom remained loyal to the kings from the line of David.

It was Solomon's son and successor, Rehoboam, who forced the final split. When the northern tribes refused to accept him as king until he relieved their tax burden, Rehoboam responded with threats of even more taxes. The tribes, infuriated, seceded from Rehoboam's kingdom. The king retreated to Jerusalem, and the period of the Divided Kingdom was begun. For two centuries, Israel and Judah would remain at odds. In the south, in the remote hill country of Judah, the people lived peacefully under David's successors for nearly 350 years. In the north, where exposure to outside threats was greater, these two centuries were turbulent. Internal coups and external attacks plagued the state of Israel until its eventual destruction by the Assyrians in the late eighth century B.C.

The kingdom of Israel endured for two centuries but was plagued by political chaos. Nineteen monarchs from nine dynasties ruled Israel, and seven of these kings were assassinated. The Temple, the house of God and home of the Ark and Scriptures handed down to Moses, remained in Jerusalem, in Judah, leaving Israel cut off from the center of its unifying religion. King Jeroboam I (928 to 907 B.C.) established two national shrines, Dan and Bethel, on the northern

Pictured above is an image of Jehu, King of Israel, prostrating himself before King Shalmaneser III of Assyria. This basalt bas-relief was erected by King Shalmaneser to celebrate his victories.

Pictured at right is the entrance to the Tunnel of Siloam, which brings water from a spring in Gihon to the Pool of Siloam. The tunnel was built under the rule of King Hezekiah to insure Jerusalem's water supply when under siege.

And Solomon slept with his fathers, and was buried in the city of David his father: and Rehoboam his son reigned in his stead. . . . And Jeroboam and all the congregation of Israel came, and spake unto Rehoboam, saying, Thy father made our yoke grievous: now therefore make thou the grievous service of thy father, and his heavy yoke which he put upon us, lighter, and we will serve thee. . . .

And king Rehoboam consulted with the old men . . . And they spake unto him, saying, If thou wilt be a servant unto this people this day, and wilt serve them, and answer them, and speak good words to them, then they will be thy servants for ever.

But he forsook the counsel of the old men . . . and consulted with the young men . . . Wherefore the king hearkened not unto the people. . . .

So Israel rebelled against the house of David.

1 Kings 11:43, 12:3–4, 6–8, 15, 19

and southern borders of Israel to take the place of Jerusalem and keep his people from making pilgrimages to that city. In both places he erected golden statues of bulls and installed non-Levite priests to serve the cult. Whether the bulls represented God or were meant to serve as a substitute for the Ark's cherubim is unknown. What is certain is that neither shrine could replace the city of Jerusalem in the hearts of the people.

The early years of the eighth century B.C. were a time of power and prosperity for both Israel and Judah. Both kingdoms seized control of territory and held trade routes; between the two kingdoms, they controlled an area nearly as great as that of the original monarchy. But by the middle of the century, Israel's fortune began to turn. In 842 B.C., Jehu won a coup and acceded to the throne of Israel. But in that very same year, the new king was forced to submit his authority to the Assyrians who had begun to overrun Israel. By the eighth century B.C. Israel's aristocratic and wealthy classes had been forced into distant exile by the Assyrians and the nation had ceased to exist as an independent kingdom. Judah stood alone.

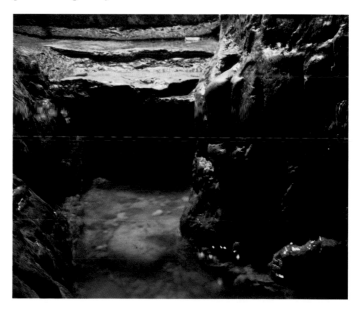

THE PROPHETS

The prophets of Judah are divided by Bible scholars into two categories. The Latter Prophets are the major prophets to whom longer books are attributed and include Isaiah, Jeremiah, Ezekiel, and Daniel. The remaining prophets are known as the Minor Prophets, only because of the brevity of their books. These "minor prophets" are Hosea, Joel, Amos, Obadiah, Jonah, Micah, Nahum, Habakkuk, Zephaniah, Haggai, Zechariah, and Malachi.

The prophetical books belong to the time of the fall of the Hebrew nation. In fact, thirteen of the prophets were connected with the destruction of the Hebrew nation and three with its restoration. Writing and prophesying just before and during the period of the fall of the Northern Kingdom of Israel, 734 to 721 B.C., were Joel, Jonah, Amos, Hosea, Isaiah, and Micah. The Southern Kingdom of Judah fell between 606 and 586 B.C. Preceding and during this period came Jeremiah, Ezekiel, Daniel, Obadiah, Nahum, Habakkuk, and Zephaniah. Connected with the restoration of the nation during the years of 536 to 444 B.C. were Haggai, Zechariah, and Malachi.

The prophets of the eighth and seventh centuries before Christ addressed themselves to kings, commoners, and the people as a whole. They were, it appears, the first to foretell the fall of Judah as a punishment for transgressions of God's law. This prophecy of national disaster was the central message of Hosea, Amos, Isaiah, Micah, Jeremiah, and Ezekiel. Ezekiel would survive the destruction of Judah and Jerusalem in 587/586 B.C. to offer the people hope for the future.

The period of the prophets covered roughly four hundred years, and the mission and the message of all of the prophets was to try to save the nation from its idolatry. The Northern Kingdom had adopted calf worship and the idol Baal. In the south, they had also turned away from the ways and word of God. Failing to turn the nations from idolatry, the prophets announced the destruction of the nations; but they also gave a glimmer of hope in that a remnant of people would survive. From this remnant would come a Saviour that would bring all nations to God. The prophets called Him "the Branch" from the family tree of David, the King of Kings, the long awaited Messiah, the Christ.

Pictured at right is The Flight into Egypt *by artist Luca Giordano. Hosea foretold the flight of Mary, Joseph, and the Christ Child when the prophet wrote: ". . . and called my son out of Egypt" (11:1).*

ISAIAH

I saiah is the first of the Major Prophets. There are sixty-six chapters in the book of Isaiah, which can be divided into five sections of roughly the same length. All of the chapters except one begin with an attack on arrogance and an appeal for justice and culminate in a hymn or prophecy of salvation.

Isaiah lived during the reigns of four kings of Judah in the second half of the eighth century B.C. During this period, Judah's fortunes changed from affluence under Uzziah to defeat and humiliation at the hands of the Assyrians.

Isaiah was most likely an educated man. His vocabulary and style are impressive, and his words have a beauty of language as well as a compassionate message. According to extra-biblical legend, Isaiah was eventually martyred (sawn in two) during the reign of Manasseh.

Chapters 40 through 55 of Isaiah are sometimes called the "Babylonian chapters." A few scholars refer to these chapters as "Second Isaiah" and believe two people wrote the book of Isaiah, but other scholars point to many similarities throughout the Book of Isaiah. Perhaps the best argument for the whole book being written by Isaiah comes in the New Testament. John 12:38 and Matthew 3:3 as well as many passages written by Paul quote Isaiah and attribute the quotes as coming from the Prophet Isaiah.

The theme of Isaiah is the translation of his name, meaning "salvation is of the Lord." The word *salvation* appears twenty-six times in the Book of Isaiah, only seven times in all of the rest of the prophets combined. Isaiah preaches that even though Judah will be destroyed, God will be faithful, and salvation for all resides in the coming Messiah.

Isaiah contains some of the loveliest passages of the Bible, and this one book is more often quoted in the New Testament than any other from the Hebrew Bible apart from Psalms. Isaiah provided the church with much of its most familiar language and imagery, including the ox and the ass at the Nativity, the Immanuel prophecy, the key of David, the suffering Messiah, the wine press, and the New Jerusalem. The Book of Isaiah has been called the "fifth Gospel" because the prophet recounts the life of the Messiah.

For unto us a child is born, unto us a son is given: and the government shall be upon His shoulder: and His name shall be called Wonderful, Counsellor, The mighty God, The everlasting Father, The Prince of Peace.

Of the increase of His government and peace there shall be no end, upon the throne of David, and upon his kingdom, to order it, and to establish it with judgment and with justice from henceforth even for ever. . . .

He is despised and rejected of men; a man of sorrows, and acquainted with grief: and we hid as it were our faces from Him; He was despised, and we esteemed Him not.

All we like sheep have gone astray; we have turned every one to his own way; and the Lord hath laid on Him the iniquity of us all.
Isaiah 9:6-7; 53:3, 6

The painting at right is the artist Michelangelo Buonarroti's representation of the prophet Isaiah. The painting is on the Sistine Chapel in Rome, Italy.

JEREMIAH

J eremiah, with its fifty-two chapters, is one of the longest books of the Bible. Unlike the other prophetic books, the text of Jeremiah is not ordered chronologically. The first half of the book consists primarily of poetry and contains the prophecies of Judah's destruction. The last half is written in prose and, although some prophecy is contained here as well, it primarily tells about Jeremiah's relationship with the kings of Judah, the final days of Jerusalem, and his journey to Egypt along with the other exiles.

The Book of Jeremiah has more biographical data than any other prophetic book, and this data provides more information about Jeremiah than is available for any other prophet (see chapters 26–29, 32, and 34–44). Jeremiah was a sensitive poet who could weep over the sins of his country: "Oh, that my head were waters and my eyes a fountain of tears" (9:1).

Jeremiah preached the destruction of Judah for about twenty years before God told him to write it down. He dictated it to Baruch the scribe who wrote the words on a scroll (36:1–4). King Jehoiakim had banned Jeremiah from the court, so the prophet sent his scribe to read the prophecy before the king. Jehoiakim became so incensed that he threw the scroll into the fire. Undeterred, Jeremiah dictated the book again to Baruch and added some prophecy that had not been included in the first scroll (36:32).

Jeremiah was continually persecuted for his prophecy. He was placed in stocks (20:2); he was thrown into prison where he sunk into the mire (32:2); and finally, he was taken to Egypt, a place he never wanted to go. Jeremiah had an unpopular message to give, and he cried out in discouragement: "Cursed be the day wherein I was born: let not the day wherein my mother bare me be blessed" (20:14).

Pictured at right is the prophet Jeremiah as depicted by Michelangelo Buonarroti on the ceiling of the Sistine Chapel in Rome, Italy.

LAMENTATIONS

The Lamentations of Jeremiah is a funeral dirge for Jerusalem. It is a short book, consisting of five poems, one for each chapter, about the siege and fall of Jerusalem in 587/586 B.C. It is from Lamentations that we have the tradition of Jeremiah as the "weeping prophet." The Septuagint, the ancient Greek translation of the Hebrew Bible, groups Lamentations with the Book of Jeremiah and prefaces the books with these words: "Jeremiah sat weeping and composed this lament over Jerusalem." In 2 Chronicles 35:25 we read: "And Jeremiah lamented for Josiah: and all the singing men and the singing women spake of Josiah in their lamentations to this day, and made them an ordinance in Israel."

Lamentations beautifully and poetically expresses profound sorrow over the plight of Jerusalem at the hands of the invading Babylonians. Jerusalem was not just the capital of Judah, it was the site of the Temple of God which housed the Holy Scriptures, the Ark of the Covenant, and the Mercy Seat. Jerusalem was where God's presence dwelt and where sacrifice could be made to Him. To lose the city was a catastrophe that would not be rectified until centuries later when the city became the focal point of God's work of salvation through the blood of Jesus Christ.

How doth the city sit solitary, that was full of people! how is she become as a widow! she that was great among the nations, and princess among the provinces, how is she become tributary! She weepeth sore in the night, and her tears are on her cheeks: among all her lovers she hath none to comfort her: all her friends have dealt treacherously with her, they are become her enemies.

Judah is gone into captivity because of affliction, and because of great servitude: she dwelleth among the heathen, she findeth no rest: all her persecutors overtook her between the straits. For these things I weep; mine eye, mine eye runneth down with water, because the comforter that should relieve my soul is far from me: my children are desolate, because the enemy prevailed.

Lamentations 1:1–3, 16

Pictured at left, silhouetted against a sunset on the island of Patmos, stands a cross, the symbol of the salvation of Jesus Christ.

Jeremiah's Scribe, Baruch, Reads from the Scroll

And it came to pass in the fourth year of Jehoiakim the son of Josiah king of Judah, that this word came unto Jeremiah from the LORD, saying, Take thee a roll of a book, and write therein all the words that I have spoken unto thee against Israel, and against Judah, and against all the nations, from the day I spake unto thee, from the days of Josiah, even unto this day. It may be that the house of Judah will hear all the evil which I purpose to do unto them, that they may return every man from his evil way, that I may forgive their iniquity and their sin.

Then Jeremiah called Baruch the son of Neriah: and Baruch wrote from the mouth of Jeremiah all the words of the LORD, which he had spoken unto him, upon a roll of a book. And Jeremiah commanded Baruch, saying, I am shut up; I cannot go into the house of the LORD: Therefore go thou, and read in the roll, which thou hast written from my mouth, the words of the LORD in the ears of the people in the LORD's house. . . . It may be they will present their supplication before the LORD, and will return every one from his evil way: for great is the anger and the fury that the LORD hath pronounced against this people. And Baruch the son of Neriah did according to all that Jeremiah the prophet commanded him . . .

Therefore all the princes sent Jehudi the son of Nethaniah, the son of Shelemiah, the son of Cushi, unto Baruch, saying, Take in thine hand the roll wherein thou hast read in the ears of the people, and come. So Baruch the son of Neriah took the roll in his hand, and came unto them. And they said unto him, Sit down now, and read it in our ears. So Baruch read it in their ears. Now it came to pass, when they had heard all the words, they were afraid both one and other, and said unto Baruch, We will surely tell the king of all these words.

And they asked Baruch, saying, Tell us now, How didst thou write all these words at his mouth?

Then Baruch answered them, He [Jeremiah] pronounced all these words unto me with his mouth, and I wrote them with ink in the book.

Then said the princes unto Baruch, Go, hide thee, thou and Jeremiah; and let no man know where ye be. And they went in to the king into the court, but they laid up the roll in the chamber of Elishama the scribe, and told all the words in the ears of the king.

So the king sent Jehudi to fetch the roll: and he took it out of Elishama the scribe's chamber. And Jehudi read it in the ears of the king, and in the ears of all the princes which stood beside the king. Now the king sat in the winterhouse in the ninth month: and there was a fire on the hearth burning before him.

And it came to pass, that when Jehudi had read three or four leaves, he cut it with the penknife, and cast it into the fire that was on the hearth, until all the roll was consumed in the fire that was on the hearth. . . .

Then the word of of the LORD came to Jeremiah, after that the king had burned the roll, and the words which Baruch wrote at the mouth of Jeremiah, saying, Take thee again another roll, and write in it all the former words that were in the first roll, which Jehoiakim the king of Judah hath burned. . . . Then took Jeremiah another roll and gave it to Baruch the scribe, the son of Neriah; who wrote therein from the mouth of Jeremiah all the words of the book which Jehoiakim king of Judah had burned in the fire: and there were added besides unto them many like words (Jeremiah 36:1–8, 14–23, 27–28, 32).

THE SCRIBE

From the very earliest of times, it was the job of certain Jewish scholars called "scribes" to copy the Scriptures in order to preserve them for future generations. Their job became especially critical after the Exile and the destruction of the Temple which had housed and protected the Word. Now, in Babylon, these scribes took on the responsibilities of priests as it became the scribes' job to copy, preserve, and even interpret the law.

Armed with this responsibility, the scribes followed precise methods and laws. Before beginning work on a scroll, the scribes offered special prayers to God. There were special religious ceremonies for the parchment, ink, and reed pens used. They then copied the words in several columns on individual parchment sheets which were then strapped together with leather thongs.

It could easily take a scribe up to a full year to prepare and copy just a single scroll.

After the destruction of the second Temple by the Romans in A.D. 70, scribes began the arduous work of establishing and copying the Hebrew Bible.

Pictured at left is a statue depicting an Egyptian scribe. The scribe is sitting crosslegged with his clothing pulled tightly across his lap to form a flat surface for writing on a scroll.

The papyrus fragment pictured above features a map of the gold mines in Sinai and dates to the eleventh or twelfth century B.C.

Pictured above is the seal of Jeroboam, possibly the same Jeroboam who was king of Judah, which dates to 1000 B.C.

Seals

Scribes and men of a high political or religious office wore a seal on a leather thong around their necks. Each seal had the person's own unique design and was used as a stamp to denote the author of a clay writing tablet or even personal items of clay. In an age when most of the population was illiterate, the wearing of the seal signified the man's status.

In 1904, a seal was discovered in the ruins at Megiddo, Israel. The inscription of this seal read "belonging to Shema, servant of Yarob'am" (Jeroboam). Scholars believe this name refers to Jeroboam II, king of Israel from 786 to 746 B.C. This era was during the time of the prophets Amos and Hosea.

Two additional seals used to seal the thong holding a papyrus document were discovered with the names of Baruch the scribe and Jerahmeel the son of the king. This find was especially exciting to scholars since both names appear in Jeremiah 36. Of course, there is no certainty that these really are the seals of these specific biblical characters, but it is possible that they are tangible evidence of an incident related in the Bible.

THE FALL OF JUDAH

Chaim Potok

King Nebuchadnezzar of Babylonia roamed at will through Syria, Phoenicia, Philistia, plundering and taking tribute. The Fertile Crescent had traded one royal thief for another. Unlike the Assyrians, the Babylonians did not engage in population exchange. Areas from which the populace was sent off remained vacant rubble.

When King Josiah died, his son Jehoahaz was placed on the throne by "the people of the land," the dominant group in Judah, landowners who strongly supported the Davidic dynasty. The Egyptians, simply to display their power over the tiny kingdom, replaced him and sent him off to exile in Egypt. The new king was Jehoiakim, an elder brother of Jehoahaz.

The prophet Jeremiah dictated a prophecy to his scribe Baruch. Nebuchadnezzar was the instrument of the anger of Yhwh. The Chaldeans would punish the lands that had mocked the LORD. Jeremiah urged surrender. The scribe read the words to the king, who tore the scroll from his hands, cut it with a knife, and threw it into the fire. Jeremiah, fearing he would be slain for treason, went into hiding. Even those in his own town Anatot, just north of Jerusalem, turned angrily upon him. Against his will, YHWH had touched his lips and given him scathing words to speak, words that condemned the chilling, soulless manner in which the reforms of Josiah were technically obeyed—and his life had become a mire of dread and loathing, dense with accusations of treason and crowded with those who sought to silence him.

Jehoiakim [ruler of Judah] probably accepted vassalage to Babylonia; we cannot be certain. He was firm in his faith in the power of Egypt; Babylonia seemed to have come upon the world too abruptly to be assured of permanence. . . .

When the Babylonians suffered a defeat at the hands of the Egyptians in 601 B.C., he threw off vassalage.

In 598 B.C., a Babylonian army appeared before Jerusalem. Jehoiakim died at the onset of the siege, possibly murdered. His son Jehoiachin, eighteen years old, ascended the throne and immediately surrendered. . . . The price of rebellion was high. The king, together with his court and about ten thousand others—scribes, soldiers, artisans, prophets, priests—was deported to Babylonia. . . . The uncle of Jehoiachin, Zedekiah, was made regent. . . . Zedekiah entered into an alliance with Egypt, now in one of her periods of revival—probably even became her vassal. Then Nebuchadnezzar marched westward. Zedekiah quickly assured him of his loyalty.

The ruler of Judah was now a vassal of two sovereigns. . . . Feeling himself strengthened by promises of support from Egypt, Zedekiah finally rebelled against the Babylonians. In 589 B.C., Pharaoh Psammetichus died. Nebuchadnezzar invaded Judah.

Jerusalem was besieged in the winter of 587 B.C. The walls could not be breached. Conditions inside the city deteriorated. . . . Plague and famine struck the city in the summer of 586 B.C. The wall was breached and the city was taken in the Babylonian month of Duzu, our July.

Zedekiah fled and was captured near Jericho. . . . About three weeks later the king of Babylonia ordered Jerusalem put to the torch. A general named Nebuzaradan arrived in Jerusalem from Babylon. He stripped the Temple of its treasures, broke down the "molten sea" and the two tall bronze pillars, and sent it all off to Babylon. On the ninth day of the Babylonian month of Abu, our August, "he burned the house of the LORD, and the king's house, and all the houses of Jerusalem. . . ." Whatever remained in the royal archives—legal texts, commercial records, literary treasures—no doubt burned as well. The city's walls were torn down. The remaining populace, except for the poor and the peasants, was deported to Babylonia.

The population of Judah had numbered about two hundred thousand people. In all, about twenty thousand were left in Judah after the 586 B.C. deportation. Thousands had previously fled to Ammon, Moab, Edom, Egypt, Tyre, Sidon, Asia Minor.

No mention is made of the sacred ark, which had been in the Temple since the days of Solomon. The humiliation of its loss may have been so painful it could not be shaped in words. We never hear of it again.

Pictured above is a detail of a bas-relief from the temple of Sennacherib at Nineveh, Mesopotamia, in present-day Iraq. The relief shows an Assyrian cart and battering ram attacking the fortified town of Lachish in Judah in 701 B.C.

EZEKIEL

Within the Book of Ezekiel, little personal information is given about its author, Ezekiel. The name itself means "God strengthens," and Ezekiel. as the son of Buzi, was of priestly lineage (1:3). Ezekiel was prophesying from exile in Babylon, since he was "among the captives" (1:1). If his words "in the thirtieth year . . ." (1:1) refer to his age, he would have been twenty-five years old when he was taken to Babylon and thirty years old when he received the call to prophesy. This would have made him about seventeen when Daniel was deported, so that Ezekiel and Daniel were about the same age. Both men were about twenty years younger than Jeremiah, who was ministering in Jerusalem.

Beginning with the opening verses, Ezekiel catches our imagination as he describes the vision that became his call to prophesy. In the fifth year of exile, about 593 B.C., Ezekiel saw "the heavens open" and a "whirlwind came out of the north, a great cloud, and a fire" (1:4). Out of the midst of this wind and fire, Ezekiel saw four cherubim, each with four faces and each with four wings, joined one to the other. Above the cherubim, Ezekiel saw the face of God, who called him to preach to a rebellious people. Ezekiel then had to eat a scroll given to him by God and which Ezekiel proclaimed was the "sweetness of honey." By eating the scroll, Ezekiel symbolically agreed to preach God's Word.

In the first twenty-four chapters of the book, Ezekiel warns the people of the consequences of their rebellious nature toward God. The remaining twenty-four chapters tell of the destruction that will befall those countries that destroyed Judah and of the promise that the exiles will return to Jerusalem. At the end of the book, Ezekiel describes the rebuilt city and Temple.

Ezekiel, like Isaiah, gives the good news that God will send the Messiah in the form of a loving shepherd, as God says to Ezekiel, "Therefore will I save my flock. . . . And I will set up one shepherd over them, and He shall feed them, even my servant David; He shall feed them, and He shall be their shepherd" (34:22, 23). For all the flamboyant behavior of the prophet Ezekiel, he gives real hope to the people in the image of the Saviour for all mankind.

Now it came to pass in the thirtieth year, in the fourth month, in the fifth day of the month, as I was among the captives by the river of Chebar, that the heavens were opened, and I saw visions of God. . . .

And I looked, and, behold, a whirlwind came out of the north, a great cloud, and a fire infolding itself, and a brightness was about it, and out of the midst thereof as the colour of amber, out of the midst of the fire.

Also out of the midst thereof came the likeness of four living creatures. . . .

And above the firmament that was over their heads was the likeness of a throne . . . and upon the likeness of the throne was the likeness as the appearance of a man above upon it. . . . This was the appearance of the likeness of the glory of the LORD. And when I saw it, I fell upon my face, and I heard a voice of one that spake.

Ezekiel 1:1, 4-5, 26, 28

Pictured at right is The Vision of Ezekiel *by the artist Raphael. The painting is based on the beginning verses of the Book of Ezekiel, in which Ezekiel sees a vision that calls him to the prophecy.*

DANIEL

The Book of Daniel relates the deportation of Daniel and his three friends, Shadrach, Meshach, and Abednego, to the palace of Nebuchadnezzar, king of Babylon. The first century historian, Flavius Josephus, wrote that Daniel and his friends were distant kin to Zedekiah, king of Judah. In Babylon, their diet and names were changed in an attempt to force them to lose their Jewish identity. The youngsters, however, resisted, and Daniel remained true to his established diet. For their faithfulness, God gave the boys wisdom, knowledge, and protection.

Daniel was written in two languages. The first chapter and part of the second were written in Hebrew, as were the last four chapters. The remaining portions of the book were written in Aramaic. Daniel was written as encouragement for the exiled Jews by revealing God's sovereign program for Israel during and after the period of exile.

The Book of Daniel contains the tales of Daniel's night in the den of lions as well as Shadrach, Meshach, and Abednego's trial in the fiery furnace—two of the Bible's most thrilling stories of faith. Armed only with their faith in God, the four young men escaped harm and became for all time indisputable symbols of faith.

Pictured below is a painting by James J. Tissot depicting Daniel in the den of lions.

DANIEL

Flavius Josephus

When therefore they [Daniel's enemies] saw that Daniel prayed to God three times a day, they thought they had gotten an occasion by which they might ruin him; so they came to Darius and told him that the princes and governors had thought proper to allow the multitude a relaxation for thirty days, that no one might offer a petition or prayer either to himself or to the gods, but that he who shall transgress this decree shall be cast into the den of lions, and there perish.

Whereupon the king, not being acquainted with their wicked design, nor suspecting that it was a contrivance of theirs against Daniel, said he was pleased with this decree of theirs, and he promised to confirm what they desired; he also published an edict to promulgate to the people that decree which the princes had made. Accordingly, all the rest took care not to transgress those injunctions, and rested in quiet; but Daniel had no regard to them, but, as he was wont, he stood and prayed to God in the sight of them all. . . . So Darius, hoping that God would deliver him, and that he would undergo nothing that was terrible by the wild beasts, bid him bear this accident cheerfully. And when he was cast into the den, he put his seal to the stone that lay upon the mouth of the den and went his way, but he passed all the night without food and without sleep, being in great distress for Daniel; but when it was day, he got up, and came to the den, and found the seal entire which he had left the stone sealed withal; he also opened the seal, and cried out, and called to Daniel, and asked him if he were alive. And as soon as he heard the king's voice and said that he had suffered no harm, the king gave order that he should be drawn up out of the den. Now when his enemies saw that Daniel had suffered nothing which was terrible, they would not own that he was preserved by God, and by His providence; but they said that the lions had been filled full with food, and on that account it was, as they supposed, that the lions would not touch Daniel, nor come to him; and this they alleged to the king. But the king, out of an abhorrence of their wickedness, gave order that they should throw in a great deal of flesh to the lions; and when they had filled themselves, he gave further order that Daniel's enemies should be cast into the den, that he might learn whether the lions, now they were full, would touch them or not. And it appeared plain to Darius, after the princes had been cast to the wild beasts, that it was God who preserved Daniel, for the lions spared none of them, but tore them all to pieces, as if they had been very hungry and wanted food.

When therefore those that had intended thus to destroy Daniel by treachery were themselves destroyed, king Darius sent [letters] over all the country, and praised that God whom Daniel worshipped, and said that he was the only true God, and had all power.

The empire of Caesar is gone; the prince of the Pharaohs is fallen; the pyramids they raised to be their tombs are sinking every day in the desert sands; but the Word of God still survives. All things that threatened to extinguish it have only aided it; and it proves every day how transient is the noblest monument that men can build, how enduring is the least word that God has spoken.
ALBERT BAIRD CUMMINS

THE
MINOR
PROPHETS

*Pictured at right is the sunrise over the
Kidron Valley in Judea.*

HOSEA

Hosea was prophesying in the northern kingdom of Israel in the middle of the eighth century B.C. He called Israel by the name *Ephraim* in his prophecies, and his message was that God loves His people passionately; even when they reject Him, God still pleads for their return to faith and obedience. Hosea depicted a God of tenderness and mercy, yet he declared that the people's rejection of God must be punished.

The first three chapters of the Book of Hosea tell the story of the prophet and his family. His wife is described as adulterous; and their three children carry the shame of their mother as evidenced by their bizarre names which mark them as sinful. Most Old Testament scholars believe that the story of Hosea and his wife is a symbolic telling of the story of God and the people of Israel. In both stories there are heartbreak, rejection, and efforts at reconciliation.

Hosea speaks of the love of God even as he prophesies the doom of Israel for its ignorance of the Scriptures.

When Israel was a child, then I loved him, and called my son out of Egypt. As they called them, so they went from them: they sacrificed unto Baalim, and burned incense to graven images. I taught Ephraim also to go, taking them by their arms; but they knew not that I healed them. I drew them with cords of a man, with bands of love: and I was to them as they that take off the yoke on their jaws, and I laid meat unto them. . . . How shall I give thee up, Ephraim? how shall I deliver thee, Israel? how shall I make thee as Admah? how shall I set thee as Zeboim? mine heart is turned within me, my repentings are kindled together.

I will not execute the fierceness of mine anger, I will not return to destroy Ephraim: for I am God, and not man; the Holy One in the midst of thee: and I will not enter into the city.

Hosea 11:1–4, 8, 9

JOEL

J oel reveals at the beginning of his book that he is the son of an unknown Pethuel; beyond that, we know nothing, except that his name means "Yahweh is God." The Book of Joel is known for the prophecy of locusts: "Blow ye the trumpet in Zion, and sound an alarm in my holy mountain: let all the inhabitants of the land tremble: for the day of the LORD cometh, for it is nigh at hand; A day of darkness and of gloominess, a day of clouds and of thick darkness, as the morning spread upon the mountains: a great people and a strong; there hath not been ever the like, neither shall be any more after it, even to the years of many generations" (2:1, 2).

AMOS

A mos is the first of the prophets whose name entitles a book entirely concerned with his life and message; and Amos was the most powerful of the biblical prophets. He prophesied during an era when Israel and Judah were at the height of their powers, and his words describe a world of wealthy and totally self-indulgent men and women who spent their days lounging on couches, eating to excess, and drinking wine.

Into this "good life" came Amos, a shepherd from the town of Tekoa, a small village southeast of Bethlehem in Judah. His prophecies, however, were directed at Israel, Bethel, and Samaria. His book begins: "The words of Amos, who was among the herdmen of Tekoa, which he saw concerning Israel in the days of Uzziah king of Judah, and in the days of Jeroboam the son of Joash king of Israel, two years before the earthquake" (1:1). Later, Amos describes receiving God's call to service: "I was no prophet, neither was I a prophet's son; but I was an herdman, and a gatherer of sycomore fruit: And the LORD took me as I followed the flock, and the LORD said unto me, Go, prophesy unto my people Israel" (7:14, 15).

Amos warned that God would destroy Israel, not because of the wealth, greed, and sloth of its people, but because of their rejection of God's Word and Law.

Pictured below are shepherds in Turkey who look much as Amos might have looked before his days of prophecy.

Many scholars date Amos toward the middle of the ninth century before Christ's birth. Recent research into the political situation described by Amos suggests that he may have lived and prophesied even earlier, since Assyria does not yet play a political role and the six nations surrounding Israel are addressed as independent states. These details more accurately depict the early decades of the eighth century.

Amos saw a God who spoke as a roaring lion, a mighty God whose wrath is terrible. The prophet's words were powerful and frightening, yet softened by his assurances that God would not abandon His people if they would only repent of their disobedient ways.

OBADIAH

The Book of Obadiah, a prophet from the late sixth century B.C., identifies itself as "The vision of Obadiah." The shortest in the Hebrew Bible at only twenty-one verses, the book gives no information about its author except his name and little clue as to the date of Obadiah's prophecies, although references seem to imply that the destruction of Jerusalem of 587/586 B.C. had already occurred. Obadiah is a less political prophet than the other twelve, his emphasis being on the future hope for worshipers of the Lord in Jerusalem. His writings are an oracle against Edom. "Behold I have made thee small among the heathen: thou art greatly despised. For thy violence against thy brother Jacob shame shall cover thee, and thou shalt be cut off for ever. In the day that thou stoodest on the other side, in the day that the strangers carried away captive his forces, and foreigners entered into his gates, and cast lots upon Jerusalem, even thou wast as one of them" (1:2, 10, 11).

Pictured at right is a statue of the prophet Obadiah.

JONAH

S ome scholars place Jonah as written in the late fifth century B.C., but little within the book confirms this date, leading other scholars to contend that the time is virtually unknowable. Jonah's book, unlike the rest of the twelve books of the minor prophets, consists mainly of prose narrative.

Jonah resisted God's call to service. He ran away, was eaten by a great fish, and was finally spewed out on dry land before he heeded God's instructions and went to Nineveh to speak God's words. Jonah did such a good job of preaching about the wrath of God that the people of Nineveh repented and escaped God's punishment. Jonah then became angry with God because He would not destroy Nineveh, and he went out into the desert to die. God sent a gourd to grow and shade Jonah; but the next day, God sent a worm to eat the gourd. Then God sent a strong east wind, and the sun and the wind made Jonah so uncomfortable that he wanted to die. God then spoke to Jonah and told him that although he had pity for the gourd that sprang up in a night and withered in a day, Jonah had no pity upon a city with more than six score thousand persons. Through Jonah, God teaches a lesson about His own power and the necessity for forgiveness.

Pictured above is Michelangelo's depiction of the prophet Jonah. The painting is on the ceiling of the Sistine Chapel in Rome.

Pictured at right is Micah as depicted in a fifteenth-century altarpiece in Ghent, Belgium. The artist is Jan van Eyck.

MICAH

Micah lived in the late eighth century B.C., was a contemporary of Isaiah, and was the first prophet to predict the destruction of Jerusalem. His words are full of foreboding: "For, behold, the LORD cometh forth out of His place, and will come down, and tread upon the high places of the earth. And the mountains shall be molten under Him, and the valleys shall be cleft, as wax before the fire, and as the waters that are poured down a steep place. . . . For her wound is incurable; for it is come unto Judah; He is come unto the gate of my people, even to Jerusalem. . . . Jerusalem shall become heaps, and the mountain of the house as the high places of the forest" (1:3, 4, 9 and 3:12b).

Micah's name is a shortened form of *Micaiah*, which occurs in Jeremiah 26:18 and translates as "Who is like Yah(weh)?" All that is known of Micah the man is his place of origin, which was Moresheth, a tiny village in the Judean foothills. Guessing from internal evidence, it is likely that Micah spoke "in the days of Kings Jotham, Ahaz, and Hezekiah of Judah."

Micah prophesied in the days of Jotham, Ahaz, and Hezekiah, all kings of Judah. Micah decried the dissolution of his own country, but he also addressed the northern kingdom of Israel and predicted the fall of Samaria. Micah's life proves that the way of the prophet is lonely: "Woe is me! for I am as when they have gathered the summer fruits, as the grapegleanings of the vintage: there is no cluster to eat: my soul desired the firstripe fruit. Therefore I will look unto the LORD; I will wait for the God of my salvation: my God will hear me" (7:1, 7).

Micah taught that the way to worship God was in humility and mercy. The book of Micah holds some of the loveliest and most cherished words in the Bible, including the prophecy of the birth of the Saviour: "But thou, Bethlehem Ephratah, though thou be little among the thousands of Judah, yet out of thee shall He come forth unto me that is to be ruler in Israel; whose goings forth have been from of old, from everlasting" (5:2).

NAHUM

Nahum prophesied in the late seventh century B.C. His book is only three chapters long and consists of a poem interpreting the fall of the city of Nineveh in 612 B.C. Nahum's words view the fall as the LORD's judgment against a cruel nation. Whereas the prophet's name, *Nahum*, means "comfort," it is violent vengeance that is portrayed in his book. "God is jealous, and the LORD revengeth; the LORD revengeth, and is furious; the LORD will take vengeance on His adversaries, and He reserveth wrath for His enemies. The LORD is slow to anger, and great in power, and will not at all acquit the wicked: the LORD hath His way in the whirlwind and in the storm, and the clouds are the dust of His feet" (1:2, 3).

Nahum is the only prophetic work called a "book" in its text. It is also referred to as an oracle or "burden," which is a term for a prophecy spoken against a nation under judgment, and as a "vision," a description it shares with Isaiah and Obadiah. Nahum's poem is seen as good news for Israel, as it describes the fall of the Assyrian Empire which has held them in captivity; but it is a short-lived hope, as Israel will fall under the rule of Egypt and Babylon, worse masters than Assyria.

HABAKKUK

Habakkuk wrote and prophesied between 605 and 598 B.C. during an era when the Babylonian armies under Nebuchadnezzar marched into and captured the Palestinian landbridge. Habakkuk lived in the kingdom of Judah; unlike the prophets who preceded him, he addressed his words to God and not to the people. Habakkuk asked God when He will fulfill His promise and bring justice, righteousness, and peace to the earth. Habakkuk describes Israel as a nation of people who do not follow God's law: "spoiling and violence are before me: and there are that raise up strife and contention. Therefore the law is slacked, and judgment doth never go forth: for the wicked doth compass about the righteous; therefore wrong judgment proceedeth" (1:3b, 4).

Sing, O daughter of Zion; shout, O Israel; be glad and rejoice with all the heart, O daughter of Jerusalem. The LORD hath taken away thy judgments, He hath cast out thine enemy: the king of Israel, even the LORD, is in the midst of thee: thou shalt not see evil any more.

In that day it shall be said to Jerusalem, Fear thou not: and to Zion, Let not thine hands be slack. The LORD thy God in the midst of thee is mighty; He will save, He will rejoice over thee with joy; He will rest in His love, He will joy over thee with singing. I will gather them that are sorrowful for the solemn assembly, who are of thee, to whom the reproach of it was a burden.

Behold, at that time I will undo all that afflict thee: and I will save her that halteth, and gather her that was driven out; and I will get them praise and fame in every land where they have been put to shame. At that time will I bring you again, even in the time that I gather you: for I will make you a name and a praise among all people of the earth.

Zephaniah 3:14–20

In chapter 3, Habakkuk is granted a vision of God's final, future judgment of all and of the establishment of God's rule over all the earth. This is the most detailed description of God in the Old Testament; and it is a beautiful and compelling portrait of the character, strength, and divinity of God: "God came from Teman, and the Holy One from mount Paran. Selah. His glory covered the heavens, and the earth was full of His praise. And His brightness was as the light; He had horns coming out of His hand: and there was the hiding of His power. Before Him went the pestilence, and burning coals went forth at His feet. He stood, and measured the earth: He beheld, and drove asunder the nations; and the everlasting mountains were scattered, the perpetual hills did bow: His ways are everlasting. Yet I will rejoice in the LORD, I will joy in the God of my salvation. The LORD God is my strength, and He will make my feet like hinds' feet, and He will make me to walk upon mine high places" (3:3-6, 18-19).

ZEPHANIAH

The central message of the prophet Zephaniah, who lived during the late seventh century B.C., was that pride was mankind's gravest sin, a sin that led him over and over again to rebel against divine authority. Zephaniah prophesied after the eighth-century prophets of judgment, such as Hosea and Amos, and before the postexilic prophets Haggai and Zechariah, who began to proclaim a coming salvation by God.

The book takes the form of a dialogue between Yahweh and someone else, likely Zephaniah himself (1:1). The first six parts of the book include a speech by Yahweh and one by the prophet; in the seventh and final part it is Yahweh alone who speaks, offering His mercy as the hope of the people for salvation.

Pictured at left is the prophet Zephaniah as painted by French artist James J. Tissot.

HAGGAI

The career of the prophet Haggai spanned only three months in the year 520 B.C. Haggai encouraged the people to rebuild the Temple after their return from exile in Babylonia. When the people cried that they were too poor to rebuild the Temple, Haggai responded that they were poor because they had not yet rebuilt the Temple. "Thus saith the LORD of hosts; Consider your ways. Go up to the mountain, and bring wood, and build the house; and I will take pleasure in it, and I will be glorified, saith the LORD. Ye looked for much, and lo, it came to little; and when ye brought it home, I did blow upon it. Why? saith the LORD of hosts. Because of mine house that is waste, and ye run every man unto his own house" (1:7–9).

ZECHARIAH

Zechariah, like Haggai, prophesied in the second year of the reign of Darius the Persian king (520 B.C.); his ministry continued until 518 B.C. Like Haggai, Zechariah was concerned with the rebuilding of the Temple. The Word of God came to him in a series of visions. "In the eighth month, in the second year of Darius, came the word of the LORD unto Zechariah, the son of Berechiah, the son of Iddo the prophet, saying, The LORD hath been sore displeased with your fathers" (1:1, 2).

Pictured at left is the prophet Zechariah as painted by Michelangelo on the Sistine Chapel in Rome.

MALACHI

In Hebrew, Malachi means "my messenger"; and although this is the name of the prophet, it is also a description of his calling. Malachi is the last of the prophets and focuses mainly on the theme of faithfulness to God's covenant and laws.

The final verses of the Book of Malachi are a conclusion to the whole prophetic canon of the twelve minor prophets. "Then they that feared the LORD spake often one to another: and the LORD hearkened, and heard it, and a book of remembrance was written before him for them that feared the LORD, and that thought upon His name. And they shall be mine, saith the LORD of hosts, in that day when I make up my jewels; and I will spare thee, as a man spareth his own son that serveth him. Then shall ye return, and discern between the righteous and the wicked, between him that serveth God and him that serveth him not. . . . Remember ye the law of Moses my servant, which I commanded unto him in Horeb for all Israel, with the statutes and judgments. Behold, I will send you Elijah the prophet before the coming of the great and dreadful day of the LORD" (3:16-18; 4:4-5).

Pictured at left is the prophet Malachi from the detail of a ceiling in Padua, Italy. The ceiling was painted by Giotto di Bondone.

Pictured at right is the city of Nazareth, the home of Jesus Christ for His first thirty years.

In Exile
Chaim Potok

They were desolate and could not be consoled. Foreign lands were regarded by them as unclean, and they felt defiled, these new Mesopotamians who had been brought from Judah to Babylonia. They had come in three groups. The first, taken to Babylonia together with King Jehoiachin in 597 B.C., had the conviction that their status was temporary and anticipated an imminent return to their land. In 568 B.C., news came of the destruction of Jerusalem. The second group of captives then arrived. A third deportation occurred in 582 B.C. There were about fifteen thousand individuals in all. Fifteen thousand. The remnant of Israel and Judah. It was a new bondage. They lived in Mesopotamia and dreamed of Jerusalem. The despair was overwhelming. . . .

They clung together. They maintained family and clan allegiances and loyalty to elders. They were careful in their observance of the Sabbath and the covenantal sign of circumcision; they rigidly forbade intermarriage—to do otherwise would have meant being swallowed by the pagan world in whose very midst they now lived. They made of their places of assembly little sanctuaries—not for sacrifice but for words.

All they had left now were words, the oral traditions and the scrolls they had brought with them—whatever those scrolls may have been; we have no way of knowing. But that they brought with them oral and written traditions we may be certain, else there would have been nothing to begin to shape into what is now the Hebrew Bible when the dark nightmare of the captivity came to an end. Scribes who had once worked in the court of the kings of Judah now copied scrolls in their homes in Babylon. One of those scribes applied the synchronized form of history writing used by the Babylonian Chronicles, which lists side by side the reigns of Assyrian and Babylonian kings, to the separate annals of Israel and Judah, unifying and synchronizing the centuries of those now dead kingdoms. They changed their script from old Hebrew to Aramaic cursive, the script of the Babylonian empire. The names of the Babylonian months of the year replaced the serial counting—first month, second month, and so on—that had been used in the period of the monarchy.

Some took Babylonian names. They selected elements from the periphery and core of Babylonian culture that would ease and enhance their lives; but nothing pagan from the world of Babylonia touched them. This small group from Judah reached sufficient critical mass to begin a process of transformation from which a new civilization would one day emerge. There, in Babylon, in the midst of a thousand pagan temples and the power of Marduk, in the world that was the birthplace of civilization for our species, paganism died for the people of YHWH.

*The Bible is alive,
it speaks to me;
it has feet,
it runs after me;
it has hands,
it lays hold on me.*
MARTIN LUTHER

THE RETURN TO JERUSALEM

Flavius Josephus

In the first year of the reign of Cyrus which was the seventieth from the day that our people were removed out of their own land into Babylon, God commiserated the captivity and calamity of these poor people, according as He had foretold to them by Jeremiah the prophet, before the destruction of the city, that after they had served Nebuchadnezzar and his posterity, and after they had undergone that servitude seventy years, He would restore them again to the land of their fathers, and they should build their Temple, and enjoy their ancient prosperity. And these things God did afford them; for He stirred up the mind of Cyrus, and made him write this throughout all Asia: "Thus saith Cyrus the king: Since God Almighty hath appointed me to be king of the habitable earth, I believe that He is that God which the nation of the Israelites worships; for indeed He foretold my name by the prophets, and that I should build Him a house at Jerusalem, in the country of Judea."

This was known to Cyrus by his reading the book which Isaiah left behind him of his prophecies; for this prophet said that God had spoken thus to him in a secret vision: "My will is, that Cyrus, whom I have appointed to be king over many and great nations, send back my people to their own land, and build my Temple." This was foretold by Isaiah one hundred and forty years before the Temple was demolished. Accordingly, when Cyrus read this and admired the Divine power, an earnest desire and ambition seized upon him to fulfill what was so written; so he called for the most eminent Jews that were in Babylon and said to them that he gave them leave to go back to their own country, and to rebuild their city Jerusalem, and the Temple of God, for that he would be their assistant, and that he would write to the rulers and governors that were in the neighborhood of their country of Judea, that they should contribute to them gold and silver for the building of the Temple, and besides that, beasts for their sacrifices. . . .

Now the number of those that came out of captivity to Jerusalem were forty-two thousand four hundred and sixty two.

THE
OLD
TESTAMENT

*Pictured at right are the ancient pyramids
at Giza, Egypt.*

THE OLD TESTAMENT CANON

Before our Bible came into being, the Hebrew canon of Scriptures had to be established. Very little is known about the authorities who established the canon of Hebrew Scriptures or about the principles and criteria that determined their sequence. The three distinct collections of the Old Testament—the Pentateuch, the Prophets, and the Writings—may well represent three successive stages of canonization. The Pentateuch's order appears to have been established long ago and has remained unchanged through the centuries: Genesis, Exodus, Leviticus, Numbers, Deuteronomy. The arrangement of books in the Prophets and the Writings, however, has only fairly recently become consistent in manuscripts and printed editions.

Many factors contributed to the recognition of the Old Testament books as canonical. The books of the Pentateuch have traditionally been attributed to Moses, which certifies them as inspired by God. The same is true for many of the books of the acknowledged prophets; their authorship guarantees them a place in the canon. Other factors include the spiritual authority the books carry in public or private readings, the fact that the books have traditionally been placed in the Temple and called sacred, and the opinions of religious leaders. For Christians, there is perhaps no stronger proof of authenticity of any book than that it is named or quoted by Jesus Himself or one of His apostles in the pages of the New Testament.

Today, the Old Testament canon exists in two main forms: that of the Hebrew Bible, which is followed by Jews, Protestants, and certain Orthodox churches, and that of the Septuagint, which includes the Apocrypha and is used by Roman Catholics and some Orthodox churches.

And the LORD said unto Moses . . . lift thou up thy rod, and stretch out thine hand over the sea, and divide it: and the children of Israel shall go on dry ground through the midst of the sea. And Moses stretched out his hand over the sea; and the LORD caused the sea to go back by a strong east wind all that night, and made the sea dry land, and the waters were divided. And the children of Israel went into the midst of the sea upon dry ground: and the waters were a wall unto them on their right hand, and on their left.

And the Egyptians pursued, and went in after them to the midst of the sea, even all Pharaoh's horses, his chariots, and his horsemen. . . . And Moses stretched forth his hand over the sea. And the waters returned, and covered the chariots and the horsemen, and all the host of Pharaoh that came into the sea after them; there remained not so much as one of them.

Exodus 14:15–16, 21-23, 27-28

Pictured at right is the Sinai Desert through which Moses led the Jews for forty years, during which time God gave to Moses the first Scriptures.

THE SEPTUAGINT

T he Septuagint is the word given for the translation of the Hebrew Bible into Greek. The word means "seventy" and is abbreviated with the Roman numeral LXX. Legend has it that in the second century B.C., Ptolemy II (285 to 246 B.C.) asked seventy-two elders of Israel to translate the Hebrew Bible into Greek. The elders are believed to have accomplished this task in seventy-two days in Alexandria, Egypt.

Today the majority of scholars accepts the substance if not the particulars of the legend and believes that the first Greek version of the Bible was created in the third century B.C. in Egypt for study by Greek-speaking Jews. The earliest manuscripts of this translation are from Qumran and are dated to the second century B.C. The Septuagint includes a number of writings not found in the traditional Hebrew canon—some are translations from Hebrew or Aramaic and others original Greek compositions. These form the Apocrypha, accepted by some Christian churches as canonical but not included as part of the Bible either by Jews or by Protestants. When the Bible is quoted in the New Testament, it is almost always from the Septuagint version, a fact that elevated its status for early Christian theologians.

In addition to the Septuagint, much of the New Testament manuscripts were written in Greek. Pictured below is a Greek text page on purple vellum, from Matthew 15:38, part of the Codex Petropolitanus, believed to be Syrian and dating from the sixth century A.D.

THE SEPTUAGINT

Werner Keller

Two unusually farsighted rulers, Ptolemy I and his son Ptolemy II Philadelphus, developed their capital city of Alexandria into a nursery of Hellenistic culture and learning, whose fame extended far beyond the borders of its own kingdoms and made it a radiant center of attraction for emigrants from Judah, among others. In this crucible they steeped themselves in the beauty of the Greek language, the only means of tasting the delights of the prodigious advances of the human mind and the human spirit. It was the international language of learning and of commerce, the language of tens of thousands of Israelites who knew no other home.

The rising generation no longer knew Hebrew as their mother tongue. They could no longer follow the sacred text in the services of the synagogue. Thus it came about that the Jews in Egypt decided to translate the Hebrew scriptures. About 250 B.C. the Torah was translated into Greek, a fact of immeasurable import for Western civilization.

The translation of the Bible into the Greek tongue was for the Jews in Egypt such an incredible step forward that legend took hold of it. The story is told in an apocryphal letter of Aristeas of Alexandria.

Philadelphus, the second of the Ptolemaic dynasty, took great pride in the fact that he possessed a collection of the finest books in the world. One day the librarian said to the monarch that he had brought together in his 995 books the best literature of all nations. But, he added, the greatest books of all, the five books of Moses, were not included among them. Therefore, Ptolemy II Philadelphus sent envoys to the High Priest to ask for a copy of these books. At the same time he asked for men to be sent who could translate them into Greek. The High Priest granted his request and sent together with the copy of the Torah seventy-two learned and wise scribes. Great celebrations were organized in honor of the visitors from Jerusalem, at whose wisdom and knowledge the king and his courtiers were greatly astonished. After the festivities they betook themselves to the extremely difficult task which had been assigned to them, and for which there was neither prototype nor dictionary. They set to work out at sea, on the island of Pharos off Alexandria, at the foot of one of the Seven Wonders of the World—the 300-foot-high lighthouse which Ptolemy II had erected as a warning for shipping far and near. Each of them worked in a cell by himself. When the scholars had completed their work and the translations were compared with one another, all seventy-two are said to have corresponded exactly, word for word. Accordingly, the Greek translation of the Bible was called the "Septuagint," meaning "the Seventy."

What had previously been made known only in the sanctuary, only in the old tongue, and only to the one nation was now all at once available and intelligible for people of other tongues and other races.

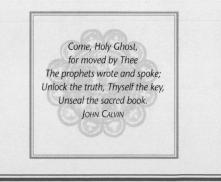

Come, Holy Ghost,
for moved by Thee
The prophets wrote and spoke;
Unlock the truth, Thyself the key,
Unseal the sacred book.
JOHN CALVIN

THE DEAD SEA SCROLLS

I n 1947, on the northwest shore of the Dead Sea, a Bedouin shepherd was looking for a stray goat when he went into a cave above Wadi Qumran and discovered several large clay pots on the floor. Inside these pots, and in others that were found in ten other caves in the surrounding area, approximately five hundred papyrus scrolls and fragments of scrolls were found. Most of the scrolls were written between 250 B.C. and A.D. 68, but the oldest scroll dates to about 350 B.C. They were written mainly in the Hebrew language, with a few in Aramaic and some fragments in Greek.

Included in the scrolls is a complete manuscript of the Book of Isaiah in Hebrew and a partial manuscript of Isaiah in Hebrew as well as manuscripts of Exodus, Leviticus, Numbers, and Deuteronomy. In fact, at least a portion of every book of the Old Testament has been found, except for the Book of Esther. There are also commentaries on the following: Genesis, Job, Isaiah, Hosea, Micah, Habakkuk, Psalm 37, and Psalm 45. Other manuscripts found include some apocryphal writings, community documents, and heretofore unknown writings.

Pictured at left are additional fragments of the Dead Sea Scroll Manuscripts.

Pictured above right is a Dead Sea Scroll that contains the Ten Commandments.

Pictured lower right are two jars taken from the caves at Qumran.

Born in the East and clothed in Oriental form and imagery, the Bible walks the ways of all the world with familiar feet and enters land after land to find its own everywhere. It has learned to speak in hundreds of languages to the heart of man. It comes into the palace to tell the monarch that he is a servant of the Most High, and into the cottage to assure the peasant that he is a son of God. Children listen to its stories with wonder and delight, and wise men ponder them as parables of life.

HENRY VAN DYKE

THE
GOSPELS

Pictured at right is an area of Galilee,
where Jesus spent His three-year ministry.

JESUS

The New Testament testifies to the life of one man, the miracles He performed, and the establishment of His church. This man was Jesus, the promised Messiah. He was the embodiment of all of the Old Testament prophecies, and His life fulfilled the promise of the ages.

Jesus lived in Judea, on the eastern edge of the Roman Empire that stretched for two thousand miles and covered most of the land around the Mediterranean Sea. He was born during the last years of the reign of King Herod the Great, who died in 4 B.C. The Gospels relate how, after the Magi told King Herod they were seeking the "King of the Jews," Herod decreed that every boy two years and under should be killed. This story allows scholars to place Jesus' birth at what would be 4 B.C. on our modern calendar.

Jesus was born in Bethlehem but raised in Nazareth by His mother, Mary, and Joseph, a carpenter. When He was about thirty years old, he was baptized by His cousin, John the Baptist, who was preaching repentance. As Jesus was coming up out of the water, He saw the heavens open, and the Spirit descended upon Him like a dove, "And there came a voice from heaven, saying, Thou art my beloved Son, in whom I am well pleased" (Mark 1:11).

After His baptism, Jesus spent forty days in the wilderness, where He fasted and prayed. He returned to the area of Galilee, where most of His ministry took place. For the next three years, Jesus, accompanied by His twelve apostles, preached, taught, and healed the people.

Jesus' message was that God's kingdom was at hand. He performed many miracles, such as feeding thousands of people with only a few loaves and fish. On the Sunday before Passover, Jesus rode into Jerusalem on a donkey to shouts of "Hosanna to the son of David." The next day, He drove merchants from the Temple and threw out the money changers and vendors with the words, "Is it not written, My house shall be called of all nations the house of prayer? but ye have made it a den of thieves" (Mark 11:17). The next day, on Tuesday, He debated the Pharisees and Sadducees and predicted the Temple's destruction (John 2:18-21).

Pictured above is artist George Hinke's depiction of Jesus.

On Wednesday of Jesus' last week, He dined in Bethany at the house of Simon the leper, where a woman anointed His head. The disciples protested the use of such an expensive ointment and suggested it should have been sold and the money given to the poor. But Jesus said unto them, "Why trouble ye the woman? for she hath wrought a good work upon me. For ye have the poor always with you; but me ye have not always. For in that she hath poured this ointment on my body, she did it for my burial" (Matthew 26:10–12). The next evening, Thursday, Jesus and His followers shared the Passover meal. As He blessed the bread and wine, He compared the bread to His body and the wine to His blood.

After the meal, Jesus and His followers went to the Garden of Gethsemane, where Jesus prayed three times for deliverance from the coming ordeal. But His disciples fell asleep. Soon Judas, one of His disciples, arrived with those who arrested Jesus. The remaining disciples fled.

When Jesus was interrogated by the Sanhedrin, He was asked, "Art thou the Christ, the Son of the Blessed? And Jesus said, I am: and ye shall see the Son of man sitting on the right hand of power, and coming in the clouds of heaven. Then the high priest rent his clothes, and saith, What need we any further witnesses? Ye have heard the blasphemy: what think ye? And they all condemned Him to be guilty of death" (Mark 14:61–64).

Jesus was brought before the Roman governor, Pontius Pilate, who questioned Him briefly. Pilate then sentenced Jesus to crucifixion. By mid-morning, Jesus was crucified on a cross on the hill of Golgotha. Within hours He was dead, having cried out His last words from Psalm 22: "My God, my God, why have you forsaken me?" The body was removed to the tomb given by Joseph of Arimathea. His ministry seemed to have ended.

But on Sunday morning, Mary and "the other Mary" went to Jesus' tomb and found the stone rolled away and an angel sitting at the entrance. Jesus appeared to Mary Magdalene and the disciples. In His final appearance, He rose up to heaven. Although the physical Jesus would be with His followers no more, He promised to send a Comforter.

THE JEWISH HISTORIAN ATTESTS TO JESUS CHRIST

Flavius Josephus

But now Pilate, the procurator of Judea, removed the army from Caesarea to Jerusalem, to take their winter quarters there, in order to abolish the Jewish laws. So he introduced Caesar's effigies, which were upon the ensigns, and brought them into the city; whereas our law forbids us the very making of images; on which account the former procurators were wont to make their entry into the city with such ensigns as had not those ornaments. Pilate was the first who brought those images to Jerusalem and set them up there, which was done without the knowledge of the people, because it was done in the nighttime. . . . Now there was about this time Jesus, a wise man, if it be lawful to call Him a man; for He was a doer of wonderful works, a teacher of such men as receive the truth with pleasure. He drew over to Him both many of the Jews and many of the Gentiles. He was [the] Christ. And when Pilate, at the suggestion of the principal men amongst us, had condemned Him to the cross, those that loved Him at the first did not forsake Him; for He appeared to them alive again the third day; as the divine prophets had foretold these and ten thousand other wonderful things concerning Him. And the tribe of Christians, so named from Him, are not extinct at this day.

Pictured at left is the Garden of Gethsemane in Jerusalem, where Jesus spent the night before His crucifixion in prayer.

Pictured above are the ruins of a synagogue in Capernaum, probably much like the one in which Jesus taught.

MATTHEW

Matthew was one of the original disciples of Jesus, and he has traditionally been identified as the author of the first Gospel in the New Testament. In the Book of Matthew, the disciple identifies himself as a publican, or a tax collector. In the Gospels of Mark and Luke, the tax collector is called by the name *Levi*, not Matthew. It is possible that the two are the same person called by different names, as was Simon Peter.

The early church attributed this first Gospel to Matthew, and although some scholars see it as anonymous, no real evidence has ever surfaced that points to anyone other than Matthew as author. Matthew was the son of Alphaeus (Mark 2:14) and was employed as tax collector in the city of Capernaum. The Jews hated the tax collectors, not only for the obvious reason of having to pay taxes, but also because the tax collectors worked for Rome and the taxes went to build Roman roads and buildings.

For many years, scholars believed that the chronology of the writing of the Gospels was that of their order in the Bible—Matthew, Mark, Luke, and John. Today, however, many scholars believe that Mark was written first and that Matthew and Luke were based on Mark. Matthew was placed first in the New Testament canon by the early church because it is a natural bridge between the Testaments with its beginning list of the genealogy of Jesus Christ beginning with Abraham.

Matthew provides the sole New Testament account of Mary, Joseph, and Jesus' flight into Egypt, an event that set the stage for the fulfillment of Hosea's prophecy that God would call His son out of Egypt. The Gospel of Matthew ends with the appearance of the risen Christ and His admonishment to His disciples: "Go ye therefore, and teach all nations, baptizing them in the name of the Father, and of the Son, and of the Holy Ghost: Teaching them to observe all things whatsoever I have commanded you: and, lo, I am with you always, even unto the end of the world. Amen" (28:19, 20).

And, lo, the star which they saw in the east, went before them, till it came and stood over where the young child was. When they saw the star, they rejoiced with exceeding great joy.

And when they were come into the house, they saw the young child with Mary His mother, and fell down, and worshipped Him: and when they had opened their treasures, they presented unto Him gifts; gold, and frankincense, and myrrh. . . . And when they were departed, the angel of the LORD appeareth to Joseph in a dream, saying, Arise, and take the young child and His mother, and flee into Egypt, and be there until I bring thee word: for Herod will seek the young child to destroy Him.

When he arose, he took the young child and his mother by night, and departed into Egypt: And was there until the death of Herod: that it might be fulfilled which was spoken of the LORD by the prophet, saying, Out of Egypt have I called my son.

Matthew 2:9–11, 13-15

Pictured at right is a painting of the disciple Matthew by artist Guido Reni.

THE SERMON ON THE MOUNT

And seeing the multitudes, He went up into a mountain: and when He was set, His disciples came unto Him: And He opened his mouth, and taught them, saying,

> Blessed are the poor in spirit: for theirs is the kingdom
> of heaven.
> Blessed are they that mourn: for they shall be comforted.
> Blessed are the meek: for they shall inherit the earth.
> Blessed are they which do hunger and thirst after
> righteousness: for they shall be filled.
> Blessed are the merciful: for they shall obtain mercy.
> Blessed are the pure in heart: for they shall see God.
> Blessed are the peacemakers: for they shall be called
> the children of God.
> Blessed are they which are persecuted for righteousness'
> sake: for theirs is the kingdom of heaven.
> Blessed are ye, when men shall revile you, and persecute
> you, and shall say all manner of evil against you
> falsely, for my sake.

Rejoice, and be exceeding glad: for great is your reward in heaven: for so persecuted they the prophets which were before you. Ye are the salt of the earth: but if the salt have lost his savour, wherewith shall it be salted? it is thenceforth good for nothing, but to be cast out, and to be trodden under foot of men. Ye are the light of the world. A city that is set on an hill cannot be hid. Neither do men light a candle, and put it under a bushel, but on a candlestick; and it giveth light unto all that are in the house. Let your light so shine before men, that they may see your good works, and glorify your Father which is in heaven (Matthew 5:1–16).

*Pictured at left is the Mount of Beatitudes
in Jerusalem, presumably where Jesus
preached His Sermon on the Mount, found
in Matthew.*

MARK

Mark is the shortest of the Gospels but is the oldest and the first written. The Gospel itself does not reveal its author, and it was Papias (A.D. 60 to 130), a bishop of Hierapolis in Asia Minor (Turkey), who first named the author of this Gospel "Mark, an interpreter of Peter." Papias then added that Mark had not followed Jesus during His lifetime but instead had later written down Peter's recollections accurately, although not always in chronological order. Subsequent tradition agrees with Papias in ascribing this Gospel to Mark.

In 1 Peter 5:13, this Mark is referred to: "The church that is at Babylon, elected together with you, saluteth you; and so doth Marcus my son." Tradition also claims he is the same Mark identified as John Mark in Acts 12:12: "And when he had considered the thing, he came to the house of Mary the mother of John, whose surname was Mark; where many were gathered together praying."

Papias and Clement of Alexandria (A.D. 150 to 215) wrote that Mark was "stumpy fingered" and that he was the first evangelist to Egypt, where he founded the churches of Alexandria and became the first bishop of that city. He had many converts to Christianity.

Most scholars date Mark before the destruction of Jerusalem in A.D. 70. Tradition held that the Gospel was composed in Rome, but this may have come about because of its association with Peter. Mark's Gospel has little that is not included in Matthew. Saint Augustine believed that the book of Mark was a shorter version of Matthew's Gospel; but Luke also includes much of the same material.

For Mark, the cross lies at the heart of the Christian message. A third of the Gospel is devoted to the last week of Jesus' life. Mark clearly shows the power and authority of Christ, identifying Him as no less than the Son of God.

And very early in the morning the first day of the week, they came unto the sepulchre at the rising of the sun. And they said among themselves, Who shall roll us away the stone from the door of the sepulchre? And when they looked, they saw that the stone was rolled away: for it was very great. And entering into the sepulchre, they saw a young man sitting on the right side, clothed in a long white garment; and they were affrighted.

And he saith unto them, Be not affrighted: Ye seek Jesus of Nazareth, which was crucified: He is risen; He is not here: behold the place where they laid Him. But go your way, tell His disciples and Peter that He goeth before you into Galilee: there shall ye see Him, as He said unto you.

Mark 16:2–7

Pictured at left is a painting of Mark at his desk writing his Gospel. The painting was completed in the fourteenth century by Guariento di Arpo.

Pictured at right is a tomb in modern-day Jerusalem that is probably much like the one in which Jesus' body was laid.

LUKE

L uke, the author of the Gospel that bears his name and the Acts of the Apostles, seemed to be less concerned with grand ideas than with people, especially those sick and in trouble. Every chapter of the Gospel reveals his concern for the poor, the sick, and the outcast. But it also reveals its author as a skilled writer, and Luke is one of the most literary works of the Bible as well as one of the most enjoyable to read.

The third Gospel is written anonymously, but ancient church tradition attributed the Gospel to Luke, whom Paul calls his "fellow labourer" (Philemon 24) and "the beloved physician" (Colossians 4:14). In 2 Timothy 4:11 we learn of his faithfulness, for Paul writes "only Luke is with me." Tradition adds that Luke was from Syrian Antioch, remained unmarried, and died at the age of eighty-four.

Pictured above is a painting of Luke writing his Gospel and the Acts of the Apostles. The artist is Giusto de Menabuoi.

Luke was clearly writing for a predominantly Gentile Christian community. He dedicates both his books, the Gospel and Acts, to a patron with what is clearly a Greek name (Theophilus). The Gospel of Luke gives a distinctive historical perspective, and he does not call his book a gospel as do Matthew and Mark but in Acts 15:7 calls it instead a "narrative account." Luke's central theme is how God's miraculous power guided the course of events from Christ's birth to His resurrection, to the beginning of the church in Jerusalem and its spread to Rome and surrounding cities, and finally to Paul's statement at the end of Acts: "This salvation of God has been sent to the Gentiles; they will listen" (Acts 28:28).

The Gospel of Luke relates some of Jesus' best-known parables, including the Good Samaritan and the Prodigal Son. Luke's Gospel follows the road to Jerusalem as Jesus' ministry moves in a purposeful direction from the provincial village of Nazareth to the holy yet rebellious city of Jerusalem. Luke's second volume, the Acts of the Apostles, reverses that direction as the disciples journey with their message of salvation from Jerusalem and out into "Judea and Samaria, and to the ends of the earth" (Acts 1:8).

THE BIRTH OF JESUS CHRIST
AS RECORDED IN THE GOSPEL OF LUKE

Pictured above is the Annunciation to Mary by the angel
Gabriel. The painting is by Fra Giovanni da F. Angelico.

And it came to pass in those days, that there went out a decree from Caesar Augustus, that all the world should be taxed. (And this taxing was first made when Cyrenius was governor of Syria.) And all went to be taxed, every one into his own city. And Joseph also went up from Galilee, out of the city of Nazareth, into Judaea, unto the city of David, which is called Bethlehem; (because he was of the house and lineage of David:) To be taxed with Mary his espoused wife, being great with child. And so it was, that, while they were there, the days were accomplished that she should be delivered. And she brought forth her firstborn son, and wrapped Him in swaddling clothes, and laid Him in a manger; because there was no room for them in the inn.

And there were in the same country shepherds abiding in the field, keeping watch over their flock by night. And, lo, the angel of the LORD came upon them, and the glory of the LORD shone round about them: and they were sore afraid. And the angel said unto them, Fear not: for, behold, I bring you good tidings of great joy, which shall be to all people. For unto you is born this day in the city of David a Saviour, which is Christ the LORD. And this shall be a sign unto you; Ye shall find the babe wrapped in swaddling clothes, lying in a manger. And suddenly there was with the angel a multitude of the heavenly host praising God, and saying, Glory to God in the highest, and on earth peace, good will toward men.

And it came to pass, as the angels were gone away from them into heaven, the shepherds said one to another, Let us now go even unto Bethlehem, and see this thing which is come to pass, which the LORD hath made known unto us. And they came with haste, and found Mary, and Joseph, and the babe lying in a manger. And when they had seen it, they made known abroad the saying which was told them concerning this child. And all they that heard it wondered at those things which were told them by the shepherds. But Mary kept all these things, and pondered them in her heart. And the shepherds returned, glorifying and praising God for all the things that they had heard and seen, as it was told unto them (Luke 2:1–20).

THE DAY OF PENTECOST

And when the day of Pentecost was fully come, they were all with one accord in one place. And suddenly there came a sound from heaven as of a rushing mighty wind, and it filled all the house where they were sitting. And there appeared unto them cloven tongues like as of fire, and it sat upon each of them. And they were all filled with the Holy Ghost, and began to speak with other tongues, as the Spirit gave them utterance.

And there were dwelling at Jerusalem Jews, devout men, out of every nation under heaven. Now when this was noised abroad, the multitude came together, and were confounded, because that every man heard them speak in his own language. And they were all amazed and marvelled, saying one to another, Behold, are not all these which speak Galileans? And how hear we every man in our own tongue, wherein we were born? Parthians, and Medes, and Elamites, and the dwellers in Mesopotamia, and in Judaea, and Cappadocia, in Pontus, and Asia, Phrygia, and Pamphylia, in Egypt, and in the parts of Libya about Cyrene, and strangers of Rome, Jews and proselytes, Cretes and Arabians, we do hear them speak in our tongues the wonderful works of God. And they were all amazed, and were in doubt, saying one to another, What meaneth this? Others mocking said, These men are full of new wine.

But Peter, standing up with the eleven, lifted up his voice, and said unto them, Ye men of Judaea, and all ye that dwell at Jerusalem, be this known unto you, and hearken to my words: For these are not drunken, as ye suppose, seeing it is but the third hour of the day. But this is that which was spoken by the prophet Joel; And it shall come to pass in the last days, saith God, I will pour out of my Spirit upon all flesh: and your sons and your daughters shall prophesy, and your young men shall see visions, and your old men shall dream dreams:

And on my servants and on my handmaidens I will pour out in those days of my Spirit; and they shall prophesy: And I will show wonders in heaven above, and signs in the earth beneath; blood, and fire, and vapour of smoke: The sun shall be turned into darkness, and the moon into blood, before that great and notable day of the Lord come: And it shall come to pass, that whosoever shall call on the name of the Lord shall be saved (Acts 2:1–21).

> The Bible is my church. It is always open, and there is my High Priest ever waiting to receive me. There I have my confessional, my thanksgiving, my psalm of praise, a field of promises, and a congregation of whom the world is not worthy—prophets and apostles, and martyrs and confessors—in short, all I can want, there I find.
>
> CHARLOTTE ELLIOTT

Pictured at left is an artist's interpretation of the Day of Pentecost as found in the Acts of the Apostles 2:2, 3.

JOHN

T he Book of John moves beyond the other Gospels in that it is the most theological of the four books. It contains the most cherished verse in the entire New Testament, the simple and direct description of Christian salvation: "For God so loved the world, that He gave His only begotten Son, that whosoever believeth in Him should not perish, but have everlasting life" (3:16). The Gospel of John shares little with the other three Gospels, which are called the Synoptic Gospels because they are so closely related to one another. John provides an independent account of early Christian memories.

In the second century, a tradition arose that the Gospel of John, along with the Book of Revelation and three epistles, were all written by the apostle John, the son of Zebedee. John the apostle was the "beloved disciple" who spoke to his followers about the deeds and words of Jesus and about His death and resurrection. John and his followers eventually moved to Ephesus. After the apostle's death, his church at Ephesus published a final edited version of his gospel.

Polycarp, who knew John in his youth; Papias, in the early second century; and later in the century Irenaeus, who knew Polycarp in his youth, all agreed that the "beloved disciple" John wrote the epistles, the Gospel, and the Book of Revelation. Internal evidence supports this conclusion since the style and vocabulary of all are similar and all share many phrases along with a limited vocabulary and frequent contrasts of opposites. There are still a few scholars, however, who believe that the fourth Gospel and the Epistles were written by different Johns.

The Gospel of John deepens our understanding of the life of Jesus by telling stories missing from the other Gospels. The book is the only source for the raising of Lazarus, the meeting with the Samaritan woman, the washing of the disciples' feet, and the doubting Thomas incident. Only a single miracle, that of the loaves and fishes, is common to all four Gospels.

The Gospel of John presents the most powerful case in all the Bible for the deity of the incarnate Son of God. John's Gospel is a testimony not only to Jesus but to the possibility of life through Him, the assurance of eternal life.

In the beginning was the Word, and the Word was with God, and the Word was God. The same was in the beginning with God. All things were made by Him; and without Him was not any thing made that was made.

In Him was life; and the life was the light of men. And the light shineth in darkness; and the darkness comprehended it not. . . .

He was in the world, and the world was made by Him, and the world knew Him not. He came unto His own, and His own received Him not. But as many as received Him, to them gave He power to become the sons of God, even to them that believe on His name: Which were born, not of blood, nor of the will of the flesh, nor of the will of man, but of God.

And the Word was made flesh, and dwelt among us, (and we beheld His glory, the glory as of the only begotten of the Father,) full of grace and truth.

John 1:1–5; 10–14

Pictured at right is artist Giusto de Menabuoi's depiction of the apostle John.

LETTERS
OF THE
DISCIPLES

Pictured at right is the Judean region of Israel.

THE EPISTLES OF PETER

T he two Epistles of Peter have little in common beyond their beginnings; 1 Peter begins: "Peter, an apostle of Jesus Christ, to the strangers . . .", and the second Epistle begins: "Simon Peter, a servant and an apostle of Jesus Christ, to them that have obtained like precious faith."

The first epistle was written in fine Greek to bring inspiration to Christians in Asia Minor who faced persecution for their beliefs. Traditionally, this epistle has been attributed to the apostle Simon Peter because it contains first-hand reminiscences of Jesus' teachings and an eyewitness accountof Jesus' crucifixion

Jesus gave His disciple Simon the name *Peter*, which is Greek for "stone or rock." Simon Peter and his brother Andrew were poor fishermen who did not own their own boat. Among the inner circle of Jesus' disciples, Peter often acted as their spokesperson. He was outspoken in his recognition of Jesus as the Messiah, although slow to understand that Jesus would have to suffer. Peter often appears weak and unfaithful; but his failures highlighted Jesus' courage and compassion, and the disciple grew stronger through each trial.

Peter was the first disciple to see the risen Jesus, and he became a leader in the young Christian church. He was the first to convert Gentiles to the way of Christ, and he supported Paul on this matter in the council of Acts 15. After Acts 15, Peter disappears from the New Testament story. James the brother of Jesus apparently became the sole leader of the Jerusalem church, and Peter traveled. He may have visited Corinth, or the areas mentioned in 1 Peter 1:1, and came to Rome shortly before his death. Extra-biblical tradition says that he was martyred when Nero persecuted the Christians in A.D. 64. Later tradition claims that St. Peter's Basilica in Rome was built over his burial place.

The second Epistle of Peter is a different matter, both in form and authorship problems. This letter takes the form of a last testament and directly claims Peter as its author. Although some scholars doubt this authorship, as early as the fourth century it has been generally recognized as an authentic work of Peter. Most believe it was written just before the apostle's death (1:14), probably from Rome.

Peter, an apostle of Jesus Christ, to the strangers scattered throughout Pontus. . . Blessed be the God and Father of our Lord Jesus Christ, which according to His abundant mercy hath begotten us again unto a lively hope by the resurrection of Jesus Christ from the dead, To an inheritance incorruptible, and undefiled, and that fadeth not away, reserved in heaven for you, Who are kept by the power of God through faith unto salvation ready to be revealed in the last time.

Forasmuch as ye know that ye were not redeemed with corruptible things, as silver and gold, from your vain conversation received by tradition from your fathers; But with the precious blood of Christ. . . .

Being born again, not of corruptible seed, but of incorruptible, by the word of God, which liveth and abideth for ever. For all flesh is as grass, and all the glory of man as the flower of grass. The grass withereth, and the flower thereof falleth away: But the word of the LORD endureth for ever.

1 Peter 1:1, 3-5,
18-19, 23-25

*Pictured above is a modern-day view of the
Jordan Valley and the Sea of Galilee.*

PETER

William Barclay

We know more about Peter than about any other of the twelve, and that may well be because of the very close connection between Peter and Mark. So close was the connection that when Peter wrote his own first letter, he could speak of "Marcus my son" (I Peter 5:13). Peter has the closest possible connection with Mark's gospel. Papias, who was Bishop of Hierapolis in the first half of the second century, was an eager student of how the gospels were written and compiled. He tells us how Mark's gospel came to be written:

"Mark, having become the interpreter of Peter, wrote down accurately everything that he remembered, without however recording in order what was said or done by Christ. For neither did he hear the LORD speak, nor did he follow Him, but afterwards, as I have said, he followed Peter, who adapted his instruction to the needs of his hearers, but had no design of giving a connected account of the LORD's oracles. So then Mark made no mistake while he thus wrote some things down as he remembered them, for he made it his one care not to omit anything that he had heard, or to set down any false statement therein."

From this information we can see that Mark's gospel is nothing other than the preaching material of Peter. It must always stand to the honor of Peter that he kept nothing back. He tells of his own mistakes, of the rebukes he sometimes received from his Master, of his own terrible disloyalty. Peter concealed nothing, for he wished to show the lengths to which the forgiving love and the re-creating grace of Christ had gone for him.

Peter was a fisherman, and it was from the boats and the nets that Jesus called him (Mark 1:16, 17). Peter was a married man (I Corinthians 9:5). His home was in Capernaum, and it may well

be that Peter's house was Jesus' headquarters when He was in Capernaum, for it was there Jesus went when He came out of the synagogue, and it was there that He healed Peter's wife's mother (Mark 1:29–31; Luke 4:38, 39; Matthew 8:14, 15).

Peter was a Galilean, and a typical Galilean. Josephus was for a time governor of Galilee and he knew the Galileans well. He says of them: "They were ever fond of innovations, and by nature disposed to changes, and delighted in seditions. . . . They were ever ready to follow a leader and to begin an insurrection." He goes on to say that they were notoriously quick in temper and given to quarreling, but that withal they were the most chivalrous of men. "The Galileans have never been destitute of courage" (Josephus, *Life,* 17; *Wars of the Jews,* 3, 3, 2). The Talmud says of the Galileans: "They were ever more anxious for honour than for gain." Quick-tempered, impulsive, emotional, easily roused by an appeal to adventure, loyal to the end—Peter was a typical man of Galilee.

> *Once you and I are face to face with the Word of God . . . we can only accept or reject it. Jesus becomes the two-edged sword that cuts right down the middle, dividing us into believers and non-believers.*
> JOHN POWELL

Pictured at right is a painting of Peter by artist Peter Paul Reubens.

REVELATION

The Book of Revelation begins in letter form, "John to the seven churches that are in Asia, grace to you and peace . . ." (1:4) and ends like a Pauline letter with "grace" (22:21). The risen Christ appears to John on the island of Patmos, off the coast of the Roman province of Asia (modern-day Turkey), and orders him to write to the seven churches and offer encouragement to the faithful and warnings of complacency. John is taken up into heaven and sees God enthroned and a lamb bearing the marks of sacrificial slaughter.

The Lamb's opening of the seals unleashes a kaleidoscope of scenes, punctuated by voices and bursts of heavenly hymnody. John is writing to seven particular congregations, but his message of warnings and encouragements are for all churches, and he claims divine authority for his book.

Irenaeus (c. A.D. 180), who was from Asia and had known Polycarp, the bishop of Smyrna (c. A.D. 70 to 150), and others of his generation, dated the Book of Revelation toward the end of the reign of Domitian (A.D. 81 to 96). Irenaeus and most later writers assumed that the author was the John who wrote the Gospel and letters and that he was the son of Zebedee. But some, like Dionysius of Alexandria writing in the third century, questioned this identification because of difference in thought, style, and language. Dionysius believed there had been two writers named John in Ephesus; and Papias (c. A.D. 140) mentions a John who was an elder as well as the apostle.

Most scholars today believe Revelation was written by the apostle John, who spent his later years in Ephesus and on the island of Patmos. These scholars date the book to the later years of the Roman emperor Domitian, A.D. 81 to 96.

Pictured at right is a painting depicting the four horsemen of the Apocalypse as described in the Book of Revelation. The artist is Edward Jakob von Steinle, who painted in the nineteenth century.

Pictured below is the Greek Island of Patmos, off the coast of Turkey, where tradition says John was exiled.

REVELATION 1:1, 7–19

The Revelation of Jesus Christ, which God gave unto him, to shew unto His servants things which must shortly come to pass; and He sent and signified it by His angel unto His servant John: . . . Behold, He cometh with clouds; and every eye shall see Him, and they also which pierced Him: and all kindreds of the earth shall wail because of Him. Even so, Amen.

I am Alpha and Omega, the beginning and the ending, saith the LORD, which is, and which was, and which is to come, the Almighty.

I John, who also am your brother, and companion in tribulation, and in the kingdom and patience of Jesus Christ, was in the isle that is called Patmos, for the word of God, and for the testimony of Jesus Christ.

I was in the Spirit on the LORD's day, and heard behind me a great voice, as of a trumpet, Saying, I am Alpha and Omega, the first and the last: and, What thou seest, write in a book, and send it unto the seven churches which are in Asia; unto Ephesus, and unto Smyrna, and unto Pergamos, and unto Thyatira, and unto Sardis, and unto Philadelphia, and unto Laodicea.

And I turned to see the voice that spake with me. And being turned, I saw seven golden candlesticks; And in the midst of the seven candlesticks one like unto the Son of man, clothed with a garment down to the foot, and girt about the paps with a golden girdle. His head and His hairs were white like wool, as white as snow; and His eyes were as a flame of fire; And His feet like unto fine brass, as if they burned in a furnace; and His voice as the sound of many waters.

And He had in His right hand seven stars; and out of His mouth went a sharp two edged sword: and His countenance was as the sun shineth in his strength. And when I saw Him, I fell at His feet as dead.

And He laid His right hand upon me, saying unto me, Fear not; I am the first and the last: I am He that liveth, and was dead; and, behold, I am alive for evermore, Amen; and have the keys of hell and of death.

Write the things which thou hast seen, and the things which are, and the things which shall be hereafter.

THE
LEGACY
OF PAUL

*Pictured at right is a painting of Paul
at his desk writing one of his letters.
The artist is seventeenth-century
painter Nicolas Tournier.*

PAUL

No single man had greater influence upon the growth of Christianity than Paul. Born at Tarsus in modern-day Turkey in the early years of the first century A.D., Paul was from a Hellenistic Jewish family who traced their roots to the ancient tribe of Benjamin. Paul, named Saul at birth, was a Jew; but unlike most Jews, he was also born a Roman citizen.

As a child, Paul likely studied at the local synagogue at Tarsus before receiving his final education in Jerusalem under the guidance of Rabbi Gamaliel. Paul became a member of the Pharisees, a strict Jewish sect, and rose to a position of some eminence. There is some historical evidence that Paul may have been a member of the prestigious Jewish ruling body, the Sanhedrin.

As a member of the Jewish elite, Paul became a vigorous persecutor of Christians; but his course was changed completely and permanently one day on the road to Damascus, where he meant to capture Jewish Christians who had fled there seeking refuge. Paul met the risen Christ on that day and thereafter threw himself into missionary work throughout Asia Minor and Greece, establishing many churches and taking upon himself responsibility for bringing the Gospel to the Gentile people. There is no biblical record of Paul's death, but tradition tells that he was martyred in Rome in the middle of the first century, beheaded during the reign of Nero. Luke, in his Book of Acts, describes Paul's vigorous persecution of Christians, and then describes his sudden and dramatic conversion to Christianity:

> Stephen, full of faith and power, did great wonders and miracles among the people. Then there arose certain of the synagogue . . . and they stirred up the people, and the elders, and the scribes, and came upon him, and caught him, and brought him to the council. Then they cried out with a loud voice, and stopped their ears, and ran upon him with one accord, And cast him out of the city, and stoned him: and the witnesses laid down their clothes at a young man's feet, whose name was Saul.
>
> And at that time there was a great persecution against the church which was at Jerusalem; and they were all scattered abroad throughout

the regions of Judaea and Samaria, except the apostles. And devout men carried Stephen to his burial, and made great lamentation over him. As for Saul, he made havoc of the church, entering into every house, and haling men and women committed them to prison.

And Saul, yet breathing out threatenings and slaughter against the disciples of the LORD, went unto the high priest, And desired of him letters to Damascus to the synagogues, that if he found any of this way, whether they were men or women, he might bring them bound unto Jerusalem. And as he journeyed, he came near Damascus: and suddenly there shined round about him a light from heaven: And he fell to the earth, and heard a voice saying unto him, Saul, Saul, why persecutest thou me? And he said, Who art thou, LORD? And the LORD said, I am Jesus whom thou persecutest: it is hard for thee to kick against the pricks. And he trembling and astonished said, LORD, what wilt thou have me to do? And the LORD said unto him, Arise, and go into the city, and it shall be told thee what thou must do. And the men which journeyed with him stood speechless, hearing a voice, but seeing no man. And Saul arose from the earth; and when his eyes were opened, he saw no man: but they led him by the hand, and brought him into Damascus. And he was three days without sight, and neither did eat nor drink (Acts 6:8–9, 12; 7:57-58; 8:1–3; 9:1–9).

Pictured at right is an artistic depiction of the conversion of Saul on the road to Damascus, painted by the Flemish artist Pieter Brueghel the Elder.

Paul is known with certainty to have been the author of Romans, the two Epistles to the Thessalonians, the two Epistles to the Corinthians, the Epistles to the Galatians, Philippians, Philemon, Colossians, and Ephesians. In addition, tradition credits him as the writer of the two epistles of Timothy as well as the epistle of Titus, also known as "The Pastoral Letters" because they deal largely with pastoral or practical matters. While these letters do have characteristic evidence of Paul's theology and philosophy, they differ from the Pauline letters in vocabulary, style, and the emphasis; thus, scholars have never come to full agreement as to whether they are to be included among the works of Paul.

Letter to the Church at Rome

Romans was written during Paul's three-month stay in Corinth in A.D. 56 or 57. He had never been to this church, nor did he found it. The letter was written as an introduction to his theology prior to his visit. It is his longest and his most formal and organized in subject. It stands at the front of all Paul's epistles and remains the most important for all Christians, for it is in the Epistle of Romans that Paul so explicitly recites the basis of the Christian faith: "For I am not ashamed of the gospel of Christ: for it is the power of God unto salvation to every one that believeth; to the Jew first, and also to the Greek" (1:16).

Letters to the Corinthians

The church in Corinth was founded by Paul during his second missionary journey when he went alone from Athens to Corinth, about A.D. 51. The journey is recorded in Acts 18:1–18. Paul was in Ephesus on his third missionary journey, probably in A.D. 56, when he wrote the first Epistle to Corinth. The second letter followed some twelve to fifteen months later while Paul was in Macedonia with Titus. The first letter contains one of the loveliest passages in the Bible that ends, "And now abideth faith, hope, charity, these three; but the greatest of these is charity" (1 Corinthians 13:13).

Letter to the Galatians

Galatians provides much biographical material concerning Paul, but it is also theologically important in that Paul proclaims the doctrine of

Pictured above is a view of the Roman Coliseum.

justification by faith alone. Although there has never been any doubt as to the author of the epistle, the recipient of the letter is less certain. Galatia is ambiguous. It could refer to a people living in northern Asia Minor. Or it could refer to the region throughout central Asia Minor, including various districts in the south that were annexed to Galatia when it was made a province by the Romans in 25 B.C. We know from Acts that Paul visited southern Galatia, but there is no evidence that he ever traveled to northern Galatia. Assuming he is writing to a church in southern Galatia, the letter would have been written before the Council of Jerusalem (Acts 15). Scholars point out that if the letter were written after the council meeting, Paul would surely have cited the decision of that council since it would have bolstered his argument in the letter. This would place the writing of the Epistle to the Galatians at about A.D. 48 and would make the letter Paul's earliest writing.

Letter to the Ephesians

Traditionally, the first letter attributed to Paul's authorship from prison is to the Ephesians. Some scholars doubt that this epistle was really written by Paul. He spent three years at the church in Ephesus

During Paul's time, the cosmopolitan city of Corinth, Greece, boasted 500,000 people, including the many travelers and merchants that came through the city's two harbors. Pictured above is the Temple of Apollo in Corinth.

(Acts 19:1–40), yet his letter is written as though the people know of him only through hearsay. He mentions no one by name, and scholars point to some words and phrases that are very much unlike Paul. Other scholars believe that this letter was like our modern form letters. The oldest manuscript of the epistle does not contain the phrase "in Ephesus" (1:1). Scholars use this omission as evidence that Paul, who was known to have written other circular letters, left space for the insertion of different place names. If, however, the letter was written by Paul while he was in prison in Rome, he would have written it at the same time as the other three letters attributed to him at this time, in A.D. 50 to 60.

The Letter to the Philippians

Also while in prison, Paul wrote to the church at Philippi, which he had founded (Acts 16:12–40) as the first church on European soil (in Greece). This is a joyful letter, even though when Paul first went to Philippi he was thrown in jail, and he now writes from another prison. Scholars believe the letter was written toward the end of Paul's life, since he contemplates his own death in the letter, and most date the epistle around A.D. 60.

Letter to the Colossians

The last letter attributed to Paul in prison is the letter to the Colossians. This was most likely written by Paul with Timothy's help: "Paul, an apostle of Jesus Christ by the will of God, and Timotheus our brother, To the saints and faithful brethren in Christ which are at Colosse" (1:1, 2). The epistle states that Paul is in prison but does not suggest where. Scholars attribute this epistle to Paul's stay in a Roman prison awaiting trial at the end of his life, which would date this letter around A.D. 50 to 60.

Letters to the Thessalonians

Paul wrote the letters to the Thessalonians while in Corinth (1 Thessalonians 1:1 and 2 Thessalonians 1:1) while Gallio was proconsul of Achaia. Gallio ruled in Corinth from May A.D. 51 to April A.D. 52. Paul had begun the church at Thessalonica in Macedonia in about A.D. 49 or 50 during his second missionary journey.

The Pastoral Letters

By the time Paul wrote what are known as "the pastoral letters" (1 and 2 Timothy and Titus), he was aged and experienced and was writing to young pastors who were facing heavy burdens.

Timothy had the responsibility for the church at Ephesus. Paul gave instructions for safeguarding the worship service and guarding against false doctrine. In the first letter, Paul also talked about the conduct befitting a minister. Timothy had to be on guard that his youthfulness did not become a liability rather than an asset. He had to avoid false teachers and greed and pursue righteousness, godliness, faith, love, perseverance, and the gentleness of a man of God.

In Paul's second letter to Timothy, Paul was writing from prison, but his letter was still one of encouragement to the young pastor. He assured Timothy of his continuing love and prayers and reminded him of his spiritual heritage and responsibilities. In this second letter, Paul reminds us that Scripture is the inspired Word of God: "All scripture is given by inspiration of God, and is profitable for doctrine, for reproof, for correction, for instruction in righteousness: That the man of God may be perfect, throughly furnished unto all good works" (3:16, 17).

In the Epistle to Titus, Paul sent advice and encouragement to the young pastor of the church at Crete who was one of Paul's closest and most trusted companions. Paul told him to appoint his elders from men who were filled with spiritual character in their own homes and businesses. Throughout, Paul stressed the necessity of setting the business of the church in order, refuting false teachers, and replacing immoral behavior with good deeds.

The Letter to Philemon

While Paul was in prison, he wrote four short letters. One of these, the Epistle to Philemon, is the shortest of Paul's letters. Paul is writing about a runaway slave, Onesimus, in an appeal to the slave's owner, Philemon, to take the slave back. Both the Book of Philemon and the Epistle to the Colossians were written during Paul's imprisonment, probably in Rome in the late 50s or early 60s A.D.

Pictured at right is the ancient theater in Ephesus, Turkey.

THE GREATNESS OF PAUL

J. B. Phillips

When I started translating some of Paul's shorter letters I was at first alternately stimulated and annoyed by the outrageous certainty of his faith. It was not until I realized afresh what the man had actually achieved, and suffered, that I began to see that here was someone who was writing, not indeed at God's dictation, but by the inspiration of God Himself. Sometimes you can see the conflicts between the pharisaic spirit of the former Saul (who could say such grudging things about marriage and insist upon the perennial submission of women), and the Spirit of God who inspired Paul to write that in Christ there is neither "Jew nor Greek . . . male nor female"!

Paul had, and still has, his detractors. There are those who say he is like the man who says, "I don't want to boast, but—", and then proceeds to do that very thing! Very well then, but let us look at his list of "boasting." We have only to turn up 2 Corinthians 11:23–27. Have any of us gone through a tenth of that catalogue of suffering and humiliation? Yet this is the man who can not only say that in all these things we are more than conquerors, but can also "reckon that the sufferings of this present time are not worthy to be compared with the glory which shall be revealed in us"(Romans 8:18). Here is no armchair philosopher, no ivory-tower scholar, but a man of almost incredible drive and courage, living out in actual human dangers and agonies the implications of his unswerving faith.

But the Letter which really struck me a blow from which I have never recovered was the one popularly known as "First Corinthians." Let me explain. I had been doing some background reading, and I was reminded that Corinth was a by-word, even in those wicked old days, for every kind of vice and depravity. The Greeks, as usual, had a word for it, and "to Corinthise yourself" was to live with the candle alight at both ends, with all scruples and principles thrown aside, and every desire indulged to the full. Because of its geographical position—Corinth was easily reached by sea and was a most important port in the East-West Mediterranean traffic—it had a very mixed population with a large number of travelers, traders, and hangers-on. It was probably not intrinsically any more wicked than any other seaport, but its reputation for sexual license had largely grown because it had been for hundreds of years a center for the organized worship of the goddess of Love (first Aphrodite and now, in Roman times, Venus). As always happens where there is such widespread sexual license, there sprang up a host of vicious, fellow-travelers—greed, blackmail, cheating, slander, perversion, and the rest.

I had a fair picture of the sort of place it must have been, and indeed of what an unlikely place it must have seemed for the founding of a Christian church, when I suddenly came across I Corinthians 6:11. Paul has just recounted some of the more repulsive sins to which human beings can sink and has assured his hearers that the Kingdom of God cannot be the possession of people like that, when suddenly he writes, and such were some of you!

I had never realized what an astonishing piece of Christian evidence this is. No one doubts that this is an authentic Letter of Paul, probably written some ten years before the first Gospel was set down. And here, to people living in this center of idolatry and all kinds of human depravity, Paul can write, "and such were some of you"! What, I ask, and shall continue to ask of my non-Christian friends, is supposed to have changed these men and women so fundamentally? The personality of Paul? The most casual reading of his two surviving Letters to Corinth will quickly show that even among his converts he was not universally admired. It seemed obvious that something very unusual had happened and was happening. People, sometimes the most unlikely people, were being converted in heart and mind by *something*. To Paul and his fellow apostles it was plainly the invasion of the human spirit by God's own Spirit. The power required to convert and to sustain the new life naturally was to Paul another manifestation of the power which God showed in raising Jesus from the dead. The "fruits of the Spirit" which Paul lists in the fifth chapter of his Letter to the Galatians are not the result of fearful effort and tormenting self-denial. They are fruits: they grow naturally, once the living Spirit of God is

allowed to enter a man's inner being.

Here then are two miracles: the transformation of human nature from within and the raising of the man Jesus from death. According to Paul's Gospel, they are both demonstrations of God's power in the midst of human circumstances and in spite of human probability.

Pictured above is the apostle Paul as painted by Rembrandt van Rijn.

THE
REMAINING
BOOKS

*Pictured at right is the River Jordan in
Israel. It was in the Jordan that Jesus
was baptized by John the Baptist.*

THE LETTER TO THE HEBREWS

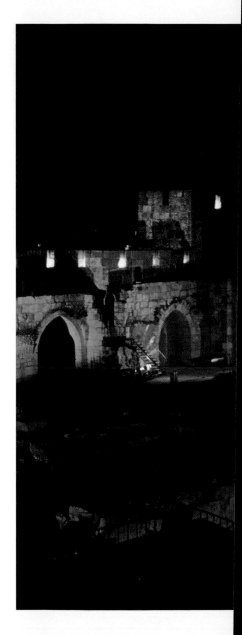

The Epistle to the Hebrews is the only letter in the New Testament other than 1 John that has no greeting, nor does it name its author. The King James Version lists Paul as the author of the epistle, but this comes from later manuscripts. Scholars universally agree that Paul was not the author.

Some scholars point to possibly Barnabas as the author. Barnabas was an active missionary and an early supporter and companion of Paul; he was also a member of the priestly tribe of Levi, a consideration in view of the considerable length devoted to the priesthood in the letter (Acts 4:36). There was a traditional association of Barnabas's name with the Epistle to the Hebrews as early as the third century A.D. from a reference in Tertullian.

Other scholars suggest the name of Apollos as the possible author, a thought first voiced by Martin Luther. Apollos was a native of Alexandria and a powerful exponent of the gospel (Acts 18:24–28).

The actual author remains anonymous, and even the date is only a guess. Since the author makes reference to the destruction of Jerusalem, the letter would have to have been written after A.D. 70 when the Romans destroyed the city. As to the place of authorship, the only clue is in the closing remark, "Those from Italy greet you," which could be assumed to have been Rome.

Pictured at right is a contemporary view of the city of Jerusalem with the tower of David and the museum of history. Although a modern-day photograph, the ancient quality of the city can be discerned.

THE LETTER OF JAMES

T he author of the letter of James claims in James 1:1 to be "James, a servant of God and of the Lord Jesus Christ, to the twelve tribes which are scattered abroad, greeting." Only four Jameses are mentioned in the New Testament: James, the brother of Judas not Iscariot (Luke 6:16; Acts 1:13); James, the son of Alphaeus (Matthew 10:3 and others), also known as James the Less (Mark 15:40 and others); James the son of Zebedee and brother of John (Matthew 4:21 and others); and James, the Lord's brother (Matthew 13:55, Mark 6:3). Tradition points to the last, a prominent figure, as the author of the epistle.

Scholars also cite the evidence provided in the portrait of James in the Acts of the Apostles, which depicts a diplomatic Jewish leader who worked to allow both Jews and Gentiles to live together in the church. They also point out that whereas the Greek used in the writing of the letter is good, it employs an inconsistent vocabulary, signs of an author writing in a second language. If the letter is indeed from James, the most likely place of its writing is Jerusalem, or at least in Judea.

The Gospels indicate that neither James nor his brothers were followers of Jesus before the crucifixion. Only after the Resurrection are the brothers mentioned among the believers who pray before Pentecost. James thereafter rose quickly in the ranks of the church. In Acts 15:13 it is James, and not Peter, who is named as the leader who summed up the deliberations of the council at Jerusalem in A.D. 49 or 50, and it was James who suggested that Jewish and Gentile Christians be allowed to remain unified without either group giving up its unique beliefs and practices.

James's leadership was so widely known that his letter identifies him only as "James, a servant of God and of the Lord Jesus Christ," and the author of the letter of Jude is identified only as "Jude, a servant of Jesus Christ and brother of James." Whereas the authorship of both of these letters continues to be debated, scholars almost universally acknowledge that the material in both letters comes from brothers of Jesus Christ.

Its light is like the body of heaven in its clearness; its vastness like the bosom of the sea; its variety like scenes of nature.
CARDINAL JOHN HENRY NEWMAN

THE FAITH OF JAMES

James, a servant of God and of the Lord Jesus Christ, to the twelve tribes which are scattered abroad, greeting . . .

Every good gift and every perfect gift is from above, and cometh down from the Father of lights, with whom is no variableness, neither shadow of turning.

Of his own will begat He us with the word of truth, that we should be a kind of firstfruits of His creatures. Wherefore, my beloved brethren, let every man be swift to hear, slow to speak, slow to wrath. For the wrath of man worketh not the righteousness of God.

Wherefore lay apart all filthiness and superfluity of naughtiness, and receive with meekness the engrafted word, which is able to save your souls.

But be ye doers of the word, and not hearers only, deceiving your own selves. For if any be a hearer of the word, and not a doer, he is like unto a man beholding his natural face in a glass: For he beholdeth himself, and goeth his way, and straightway forgetteth what manner of man he was.

But whoso looketh into the perfect law of liberty, and continueth therein, he being not a forgetful hearer, but a doer of the work, this man shall be blessed in his deed.

What doth it profit, my brethren, though a man say he hath faith, and have not works? can faith save him? If a brother or sister be naked, and destitute of daily food, And one of you say unto them, Depart in peace, be ye warmed and filled; notwithstanding ye give them not those things which are needful to the body; what doth it profit?

Even so faith, if it hath not works, is dead, being alone. Yea, a man may say, Thou hast faith, and I have works: show me thy faith without thy works, and I will show thee my faith by my works.

Thou believest that there is one God; thou doest well: the devils also believe, and tremble. But wilt thou know, O vain man, that faith without works is dead (James 1:1, 17–25; 2:14–20)?

Pictured above is artist James J. Tissot's painting of James.

JUDE

The Epistle of Jude relates the crisis of the new church. Beginning with the believers' common salvation, Jude then challenges them to contend for the faith. False teachers had crept into the church and used God's grace as a license to do as they pleased. Jude reminded them that God took Israel to account regarding Sodom and Gomorrah, and Christians should also be faithful.

General, although not complete, agreement exists among biblical scholars that the author of Jude was Judas, the brother of Jesus. Textual evidence in both Matthew (13:55, 56) and Mark (6:3) seems to support this claim. And within the text of Jude, the author refers to himself as the brother of James, who was known to be Jesus' brother.

Jude was accepted as authentic and quoted by the early church fathers. By the last quarter of the second century, it was accepted as part of Scripture by leaders such as Tertullian and Origen. The Book of Jude closes with the greatest doxology in the Bible, and one quoted in many churches today at the end of the service.

Jude, the servant of Jesus Christ, and brother of James, to them that are sanctified by God the Father, and preserved in Jesus Christ, and called: Mercy unto you, and peace, and love, be multiplied. Beloved, when I gave all diligence to write unto you of the common salvation, it was needful for me to write unto you, and exhort you that ye should earnestly contend for the faith which was once delivered unto the saints. For there are certain men crept in unawares, who were before of old ordained to this condemnation, ungodly men, turning the grace of our God into lasciviousness, and denying the only Lord God, and our Lord Jesus Christ. Keep yourselves in the love of God, looking for the mercy of our Lord Jesus Christ unto eternal life. And of some have compassion, making a difference: And others save with fear, pulling them out of the fire; hating even the garment spotted by the flesh.

Now unto Him that is able to keep you from falling, and to present you faultless before the presence of His glory with exceeding joy, To the only wise God our Saviour, be glory and majesty, dominion and power, both now and ever. Amen (1:1–4, 21–25).

Pictured at right is the apostle Jude, the brother of Jesus and James, as depicted by artist Anthonis van Dyck.

THE
HOLY
BIBLE

*Pictured at right is a stirring portrait of the
Nativity by artist Sandro Botticelli.*

THE CHRISTIAN BIBLE

T
he Christian Bible that we have today owes its existence to
many people throughout history. The first three hundred years
after the death of Christ saw the greatest persecution of
Christians in the history of mankind. So many were put to death, it is
a miracle that the faith survived at all, and it is a testament that God
does indeed work in mysterious ways His wonders to perform.

After the death of Jesus Christ, His followers began establishing
churches throughout the Roman Empire. The letters of Paul, Peter,
and others were meticulously copied and passed around to all of the
churches. But in A.D. 64, the Emperor Nero ushered in an era of
unprecedented persecutions of Christians. He blamed them for setting
fire to the city, the excuse for a massacre of most of the Christian community in Rome. After Nero, Emperor Domitian in A.D. 95 ordered
the death of all Roman subjects who refused to recognize the Roman
emperor as a god. By A.D. 303, under Emperor Diocletian, the persecutions peaked as Diocletian was determined to rid the
empire of all Christians. He imprisoned all of the
clergy, burned the churches, and burned all copies of
the Scriptures he could find. Many of the Apostolic
Fathers (early church leaders, including Ignatius,
Clement of Rome, Polycarp, and Hermas, whose
writings on the early church are of deep importance),
were martyred during this long period of persecution.

The Emperor Diocletian had divided the empire
into East and West sectors. When Constantine came
to rule in the West, he invaded Italy to claim all of
the Roman Empire under his rule. Preparing for the
battle with Maxentius, ruler of the East Roman
Empire, Constantine was at the Milvian Bridge and,
according to legend, saw a vision of a flaming cross
shining in the sky. Constantine was victorious that
day, defeating Maxentius in battle; and Constantine
took the vision of the cross as evidence of the power
of Christianity.

In A.D. 313, Constantine, in the Edict of Milan, declared freedom of worship for all religions in the Roman Empire. In addition, he declared Sunday as a day of rest, restored the churches, and exempted Christians from participating in pagan sacrifices. In later life, Constantine became a Christian and was baptized.

Because Constantine wanted to have a Christian Bible produced, he commissioned Eusebius of Caesarea to produce fifty Bibles for use in Constantinople. First, Eusebius had to determine which of the writings to include in the Bible; and to do so, he established three classes of Christian texts. First were those writings that were already universally accepted as sacred. These included the four Gospels, the Acts of the Apostles, the thirteen letters attributed to Paul, 1 John, and 1 Peter. The second group of texts were those that had some incredulous but were generally regarded as sacred and are now a part of the New Testament. These were James, 2 Peter, Jude, 2 and 3 John, Hebrews, and Revelation. The third group of texts were those that Eusebius rejected. Some of these are now a part of the Apocrypha.

THE LATIN BIBLE

As Latin replaced Greek as the language of the empire, there arose the need for a Latin Old Testament to replace the Greek Septuagint, and for a Christian Canon of writings. The New Testament manuscripts were written in Greek, so they and the Septuagint were translated into Latin. This task fell to Eusebius Hieronymous, known in English as Jerome.

Jerome was born in about A.D. 346 into a wealthy Roman home. His parents were Christians, and Jerome received a classical Roman education. He built up his own library by copying manuscripts and became a monk, lived in a cave, and filled his days with prayer. In A.D. 379, Jerome left his solitary life and went to Rome, where he became the secretary to Pope Damasus. The pope commissioned Jerome to produce a Latin version of the Bible. After one year, Jerome had completed the New Testament and set to work on the Old Testament, which he completed in A.D. 405. Jerome's translation is known as the Latin Vulgate. This is the Bible that traveled to Western Europe.

Pictured at left is Jerome, who translated the Bible into Latin and formed the basis for the Wycliffe Bible, the first Bible to be translated into English. The painting is by artist Domenico Ghirlandaio.

THE PRINTED BIBLE

During the first 1400 years after the death of Christ, Bibles were produced completely by hand. They were copied by monks, working in monasteries, with quill pens and ink, sometimes going through one hundred pens a day. The copying was onto parchment, which was made from animal skins. During the medieval period, illuminated manuscripts were popular. These are manuscripts that are "lit up" with colorful and intricate illustrations. Initial capital letters might grow into fanciful paintings depicting the history of the time of the writing of the manuscript. Some monks used gold leaf, which is actual gold that has been hammered into paper-thin strips. The monk usually then passed off the manuscript to another artist who would lay in the colored pigments, creating sometimes breathtakingly beautiful pages.

Medieval Bibles are also known for their elaborate bindings. Often they were covered in leather with intricate stamping or tooling. These Bibles were all, of course, for use only in cathedrals and monasteries and removed from storage only for use in the service.

In 1390, a son was born to a patrician family in Mainz, Germany, who would change bookmaking and thus the Scriptures forever. The child was named Johann Gutenberg and trained as a goldsmith. In 1454, Gutenberg borrowed a great deal of money and began printing small publications in his hometown of Mainz. Little is known about his printing press, but the ink he used is similar in composition to oil-based paint and has never lost its luster. He printed on a rag-based paper.

In 1454, Gutenberg exhibited sample pages of his Bible at a Frankfurt trade fair. At the fair was the future Pope Pius II, who praised the Bible, mainly because it could be read without glasses. In 1455, Gutenberg had an argument with his partner Johann Fust, who subsequently sued Gutenberg. Fust won the case and was awarded ownership of Gutenberg's press. Fust finished production on the 180 Bibles that had been sold at the fair and collected all of the proceeds. Today, only forty-eight of the Gutenberg Bibles survive.

The invention of the printing press made the Scriptures accessible to all and fomented the Protestant Reformation, which insisted that each person could interpret the Bible without the intervention of the church.

Pictured at right is a replica of the printing press invented by Gutenberg.

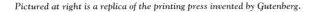

THE BIBLE IN ENGLISH

T he first complete English Bible was the work of John Wycliffe and his students. It was not a translation from the original languages; those manuscripts had not yet been discovered. Wycliffe and his students translated Jerome's Latin Vulgate of A.D. 405 into the English of the period. It is not clear whether Wycliffe did any translation himself, but he was certainly the guiding force behind the work. Wycliffe's was *the* Bible in English until 1396, when John Purvey revised the cramped style of the Old Testament and brought the style more in keeping with Wycliffe's New Testament.

The man who laid the foundation for the Bible in English was William Tyndale, whose translation of the New Testament was published at Worms, Germany, in 1525 and was the first printed edition of the New Testament in English. Wycliffe's Bible had never been printed and suffered from errors since it was a translation of the Latin Vulgate. Tyndale later translated about half of the Old Testament and would have translated the complete Old Testament had he lived. But he was captured by his enemies in 1535 and burned at the stake in 1536. The legacy he left, that of simplicity of diction and rhythmic phrases, provided the pattern and much of the substance of later editions.

Pictured at right are the Old Testament manuscripts of the Douay Bible.

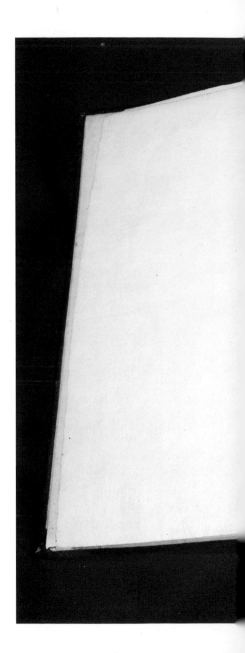

THE
HOLIE BIBLE
FAITHFVLLY TRANS-
LATED INTO ENGLISH,
OVT OF THE AVTHENTICAL
LATIN.

Diligently conferred with the Hebrew, Greeke,
and other Editions in diuers languages.

With ARGVMENTS of the Bookes, and Chapters:
ANNOTATIONS: TABLES: and other helpes,
for better vnderstanding of the text : for difcouerie of
CORRVPTIONS in fome late tranflations: and
for clearing CONTROVERSIES in Religion.

BY THE ENGLISH COLLEGE OF DOWAY.

Haurietis aquas in gaudio de fontibus Saluatoris.   Ifaiæ. 12.
You shal draw waters in ioy out of the Sauiours fountaines.

Printed at Doway by LAVRENCE KELLAM,
at the figne of the holie Lambe,
M. DC. IX.

The task of completing the translation fell to Miles Coverdale. The first complete Bible in English was printed in 1535. Coverdale lacked the scholarship to translate the Bible from its original languages; and in his dedication, he stated that he relied heavily on the work of earlier translations, including Tyndale's.

Other English translations and revisions appeared during this period. In 1540, Coverdale printed the Great Bible to meet Henry VIII's injunctions of 1538 that a copy "of the whole Bible of the largest volume in English be set up in churches." Shakespeare used the Geneva Bible, which was brought to America on the *Mayflower* by the Puritans in 1620. The Geneva Bible is also called the "Breeches Bible" because of the translation of Genesis 3:7, "They sewed figtree leaves together, and made themselves breeches." The Roman Catholic English version of the New Testament, prepared by members of the English College at Douay, was published in Rheims, France, in 1582. Their version of the Old Testament was published in 1609.

All of these versions and translations were leading up to what has been called "the only classic ever created by a committee." The Authorized or King James Version of the Holy Bible was printed in 1611, and the translators consisted of men of different faiths and orders, but all devoted to the task of making the Word of God accessible to English readers.

From a literary point of view, it is a miracle that these scholars could have produced such a consistently beautiful book. They built upon the simple beauty and the spiritual fervor of the original Hebrew Scriptures. They kept the vigor of the Greek, which carried the Christian message of the New Testament. They lived in an age of faith and had a conviction that they were handling the inspired Word of God. And they wrote at a time when the English language was at the highest point of strength and beauty it had yet reached. Poetry was in the air, and the English speech had a natural stateliness which it has since lost. Many of its phrases have enriched everyday speech, and to be ignorant of it is to be out of touch with the greatest single influence in both the literature and life of the English-speaking world.

Pictured below is the elaborate frontispiece of a sixteenth-century Bible.

FROM THE KING JAMES BIBLE, 1611

Lay not up for yourselves treasures upon earth, where moth and rust doth corrupt, and where thieves break through and steal: But lay up for yourselves treasures in heaven, where neither moth nor rust doth corrupt, and where thieves do not break through nor steal: For where your treasure is, there will your heart be also. The light of the body is the eye: if therefore thine eye be single, thy whole body shall be full of light. But if thine eye be evil, thy whole body shall be full of darkness. If therefore the light that is in thee be darkness, how great is that darkness! No man can serve two masters: for either he will hate the one, and love the other; or else he will hold to the one, and despise the other. Ye cannot serve God and mammon. Therefore I say unto you, Take no thought for your life, what ye shall eat, or what ye shall drink; nor yet for your body, what ye shall put on. Is not the life more than meat, and the body than raiment? Behold the fowls of the air: for they sow not, neither do they reap, nor gather into barns; yet your heavenly Father feedeth them. Are ye not much better than they? Which of you by taking thought can add one cubit unto his stature? And why take ye thought for raiment? Consider the lilies of the field, how they grow; they toil not, neither do they spin: And yet I say unto you, That even Solomon in all his glory was not arrayed like one of these. Wherefore, if God so clothe the grass of the field, which today is, and tomorrow is cast into the oven, shall He not much more clothe you, O ye of little faith? Therefore take no thought, saying, What shall we eat? or, What shall we drink? or, Wherewithal shall we be clothed? (For after all these things do the Gentiles seek:) for your heavenly Father knoweth that ye have need of all these things. But seek ye first the kingdom of God, and His righteousness; and all these things shall be added unto you. Take therefore no thought for the morrow: for the morrow shall take thought for the things of itself. Sufficient unto the day is the evil thereof.

Ask, and it shall be given you; seek, and ye shall find; knock, and it shall be opened unto you: For every one that asketh receiveth; and he that seeketh findeth; and to him that knocketh it shall be opened. Or what man is there of you, whom if his son ask bread, will he give him a stone? Or if he ask a fish, will he give him a serpent? If ye then, being evil, know how to give good gifts unto your children, how much more shall your Father which is in heaven give good things to them that ask Him? Therefore all things whatsoever ye would that men should do to you, do ye even so to them: for this is the law and the prophets.

Enter ye in at the strait gate: for wide is the gate, and broad is the way, that leadeth to destruction, and many there be which go in thereat: Because strait is the gate, and narrow is the way, which leadeth unto life, and few there be that find it. Beware of false prophets, which come to you in sheep's clothing, but inwardly they are ravening wolves. Ye shall know them by their fruits. Do men gather grapes of thorns, or figs of thistles? Even so every good tree bringeth forth good fruit; but a corrupt tree bringeth forth evil fruit. A good tree cannot bring forth evil fruit, neither can a corrupt tree bring forth good fruit. Every tree that bringeth not forth good fruit is hewn down, and cast into the fire. Wherefore by their fruits ye shall know them (Matthew 6:19–34, 7:7-20).

INDEX

PHOTOGRAPHY CREDITS